A BEGINNER'S BOOK
OF
NEEDLEPOINT
AND
EMBROIDERY

A BEGINNER'S BOOK OF NEEDLEPOINT AND EMBROIDERY

Xenia Ley Parker

Illustrated with drawings and photographs by the author

DODD, MEAD & COMPANY · NEW YORK

Library of Congress Cataloging in Publication Data

Parker, Xenia Ley.
  A beginner's book of needlepoint and embroidery.

  Includes index.
  SUMMARY: Discusses the history, materials, tools,
patterns, procedures, and stitches of embroidery and
needlepoint.
    1. Canvas embroidery—Juvenile literature.
2. Needlework—Juvenile literature. [1. Canvas
embroidery. 2. Needlework] I. Title.
TT778.C3P37   746.4'4   74-25511
ISBN 0-396-07066-3

CONTENTS

INTRODUCTION

Welcome to the world of needlepoint and embroidery. Among the most popular of the hand crafts, they are sure to please, with their basic stitches and attractive results. You'll find that you need no experience with a needle and thread to build a firm foundation while learning and enjoying these creative activities. The ease with which you'll come to know the fundamentals should be a pleasant surprise.

The first few stitches, in each type of work, are enough to allow you to start a new friendship. As you develop your new versatility with a needle and yarn, your imagination will take over. Whether you want to add a sparkling touch of decoration to a piece of clothing or go off on your own to plan a pictorial scene for a pillow, you'll soon be able to, with just a bit of practice.

1

NEEDLECRAFT, PAST AND PRESENT

Decorative stitchery has existed for such a long time that there are mentions of it in the Bible and in many other ancient records that are the beginning of history as we know it. There are also examples of stitched works that are thousands of years old, although often only the smallest fragments survive, as the cloth that the stitches are made on does not always last as well as the stitches themselves do.

The Persians of long ago thought that the cloth they wove was too rough and plain to be attractive, so they covered as much of it as they could with embroidery. An added benefit of the newly beautiful fabric was that it became longer wearing because it was strengthened by the many threads of the finely made stitches.

Chinese embroidery became world famous, with its perfection of technique in silk threads on silk cloth. The shimmering secret of the manufacture of silk was jealously guarded by the Chinese, who were the only ones to cultivate silkworms for many years. The little creatures became known to the Emperor Justinian of Constantinople in the early Middle Ages, when silkworm eggs were smuggled into the Western world in the hollowed-out handles of walking sticks.

Although the method of making silk cloth became known in Europe, its origins weren't forgotten and many of the designs used were inspired by the Chinese works. Silk remnants found in the tomb of Charlemagne, who was crowned Holy Roman Emperor on Christmas Day in the year 800, contain the purely Oriental elephant motifs, carefully stitched within medallion shapes, another Oriental design.

Franco-Flemish embroidered textile, c. 1430-1440. Roundel: St. Martin and the Brigands. Silk and metal thread on linen. Diameter 6½". *Courtesy, The Metropolitan Museum of Art, The Cloisters Collection, Purchase, 1947.*

Much of our tradition in stitchery, however, comes from England. At the time of the Saxons, a people who lived there, the arts of embroidery were widely known and used. King Aethelstan, who lived in the tenth century, had four sisters who were renowned for their talents in stitched works. After the Normans, led by William the Conqueror, invaded England in 1066, their feats in battle were commemorated in a series of large embroidered panels that are known as the Bayeux Tapestry. Actually, only their cloth is woven—in a true tapestry the entire design is woven—and the pictures of the events are stitched. They are thought to have been done by, or at least directed in work by, William's wife, Queen Mathilda. They contain a detailed pictorial presentation of not only the battles, but the quality of life at the time.

By the time of Henry VIII, it was thought that a well-brought-up young girl must have a good knowledge of needlework, along with other talents. This was demonstrated in the artistry of samplers, hangings, decorations,

American, early 18th century. Bedspread, linen, embroidered in crewels, linen, and wool. *Courtesy, The Metropolitan Museum of Art, Gift of George Coe Graves, 1924.*

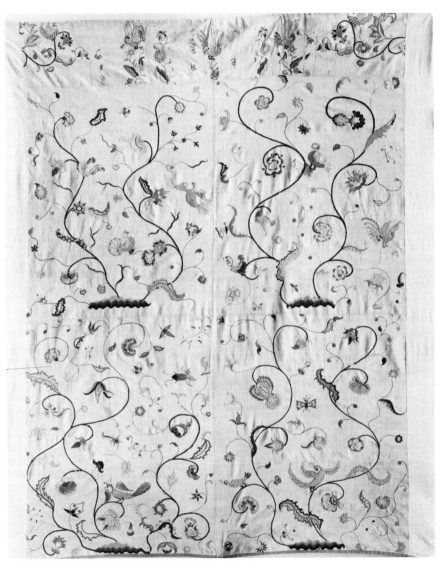

and religious works. Indeed, Henry's daughter Elizabeth, who later became Queen, was quite good at embroidery and her later rivalry with Mary, Queen of Scots, extended beyond politics and court intrigue into the question of who was the finer artist with a needle.

By the middle of the seventeenth century, a new style began to take hold. It was called Jacobean and had an exotic flavor, depicting birds, fruits, flowers, trees, and animals in strange bumpy landscapes. The small mounds at the base of growing things in these scenes are well known as distinctive features of the style. These works were further stimulated by newly imported block-printed fabrics from India that had other unusual motifs and subjects. The interesting part of these fabrics is that their designs had actually been copied in India from English needlework sent there earlier in the century. As the Indian workers adapted these patterns for their own fabric designs, the structure of the printing blocks and the personal viewpoints of the Indian artists changed the English motifs so much that for years they were not recognized as such.

Stitcheries became larger in scope and design as art needlework developed. Designs included pictures and scenes of the gentle life. Along with the women who did fine work to pass their leisure hours and fill their houses with precious stitched heirlooms, men were often the designers and executors of needlework. They were the members of the craft guilds that did these works on a commercial basis, and no women were allowed to belong.

America became a center of activity as the colonies were explored and settled in the seventeenth century. When the *Mayflower* left England on its perilous journey it carried the creative experiences and abilities of its passengers as well as their hopes for a bright future in the new land. One of the forms that was brought over and became popular among the children of the colonies was the making of finely stitched samplers.

The samplers were meant to teach and display a variety of embroidery stitches. Through them, the sewers also mastered the alphabet and numbers while learning the stitches. As the life in the colonies developed in its own way, the samplers also changed and became more distinctly American. The handwoven linen backing was covered with fewer different stitches and colors than those made in Europe. The use of other fabrics, such as twilled linen, with a texture unlike the homespun kind, wasn't

English, first half 18th century. Panel for a handscreen (one of a pair), embroidered in colored wool in tent stitch, wool on canvas, A. Shepherd. *Courtesy, The Metropolitan Museum of Art, Rogers Fund, 1910*

really widespread until the time of the Revolution when the production of commercially made cloth of many types began for the first time. Up until then, American manufacture was discouraged by the English, who planned to sell their own finished goods in America while the raw materials were to be sent to England in return.

Stitched works were mostly made by women and children, who devoted many hours to the creation of articles for home and family use. Their accomplishments with needle and thread added a lot of beauty to the often

Next unto God Dear Parents I addrefs
Myself to you in Humble Thankfulnefs
For all your Care and Charge on me bestowed
The means of Learning unto me allowed
Go on I Pray and Let me still Pursue
Those Golden arts the Vulgar never knew

Caroline Curtis
workd this sampler
aged 8 years
18   24

English, 19th century. Sampler: natural color, embroidered in shades of green, blue, and tan silk. Silk on linen. Caroline Curtis worked this sampler, aged 8 years, 1824. *Courtesy, The Metropolitan Museum of Art, Rogers Fund, 1912*

rustic nature of their dwellings. Needlecrafts were used in many ways, including the comfort of rugs and quilts, as picture arts in stitched scenes, to add a fine touch to the clothing and accessories of both men and

14

women, and to express the new patriotism. Martha Washington, whose husband naturally became the subject of many stitched portraits, made many sewn works, including seat covers on heavy canvas for twelve chairs in their Mount Vernon home.

American stitchers became more adventurous than their English cousins and made up new designs and patterns to suit themselves, instead of repeating often-used ones. As people from many countries settled in the newly formed United States, their different backgrounds added much to the pool of designs and styles that was America.

By the nineteenth century the popularity of needlework was widespread and increased with the introduction of "Berlin Work." This is done in what we would probably call needlepoint, with painted designs that originally came from Berlin. Later, wool yarns colored with aniline dyes came from the same source. The paper patterns for the work included art works and other designs, with the colors filled in, a new feature. All the needleworker had to do was to follow the printed squares, each standing for one stitch, to create the design on the canvas. Although the repetition of the same ideas in preplanned designs like these left little to the individual's imagination, these works introduced a great number of people to the pleasures of stitchery.

Today, stitchery of all kinds is reaching an ever-growing audience. Needleworks hang in museums and galleries as well as giving a welcome warmth and beauty to home and surroundings. You can choose from several techniques for a personal touch. *Needlepoint*, sometimes called canvas work, is actually a form of embroidery done on an open-meshed canvas backing with a blunt needle and yarn. *Bargello* is a variation of needlepoint where larger stitches in bright colors are used in rhythmic patterns that rise and fall as they move across the canvas. *Crewel embroidery* is usually done on linen but can be worked on almost any fabric, from denim to silk, as long as it's stretched in a hoop and stitched with wool yarn and a sharp-pointed needle. *Embroidery*, as a more general term, includes decorative stitchery done on any fabric with embroidery floss or almost any kind of thread or yarn. Whichever method you choose, you're in for a treat. The colors of yarn and thread alone are often enough to set your imagination to work.

One of the most interesting ways to start stitching, in any technique, is

**American, c. 1795, Bristol, Rhode Island, by Patty Coggeshall, born 1780.
Sampler: embroidered in vari-colored silks in satin stitch, petit point, and
rococo stitch, silk on canvas.** *Courtesy, The Metropolitan Museum of Art,
Rogers Fund, 1913*

to make a sampler. It can be made up of any and all stitches that you want
to try. It will give you an idea of which stitches you enjoy doing and would
want to execute on a larger-scale project. As a sampler progresses you'll

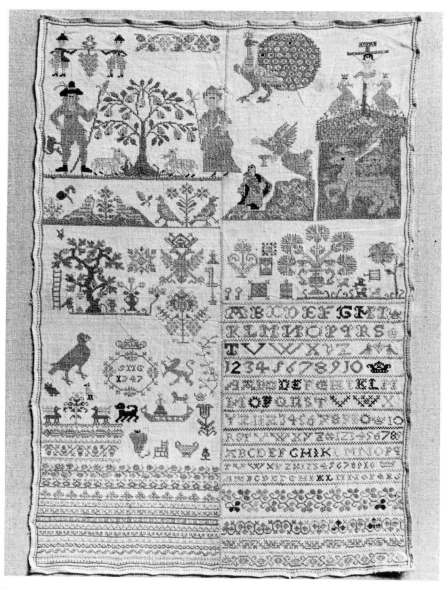

German, 18th century. Sampler, silk on linen, dated 1747. *Courtesy, The Metropolitan Museum of Art, Fischbach Collection, 1909*

know how to do many stitches and when it's finished you'll discover that the sampler itself is an adventure in stitchery, worthy of hanging on a wall, like the samplers of old.

2

CANVAS AND FABRIC BACKINGS
TO STITCH

A basic requirement of needlepoint and embroidery is a suitable backing to work the stitches onto so that they form easily and well.

Needlepoint Canvas

In needlepoint, specially made, open-meshed canvases are used. They come in many qualities, sizes, and widths and are made of cotton, linen, hemp, or flax, the most usual being cotton or linen. The individual threads of the canvas are woven together so that you can see evenly spaced open holes in the canvas. These open spaces are filled with yarn as the stitching proceeds and each crossing of canvas threads is called a *mesh*. The size of the space is determined by the number of mesh per inch, so that a canvas called 10-mesh has ten thread crossings per inch, a 12-mesh has twelve crossings, and so on. The size of the mesh is very important, as it tells you which kind of needle and yarn to use.

The way that the mesh are woven into canvas gives us two kinds of needlepoint canvas. One is called *mono canvas*, which has a simple one-thread weave, where each thread crosses one other thread, with equal spacing both up and down and from side to side. In a mono canvas, the number of mesh refers to the actual number of threads that you can count in an inch. The second type of canvas is called *penelope canvas* and is woven with a double thread. It was a French invention of 1865. In penelope canvas, the mesh or crossing threads are double, or composed of two

18

Needlepoint canvases, in mono and penelope weaves

threads each. In this type of canvas, a 10-mesh would have twenty actual threads in an inch. To show this difference, when referring to the mesh, some penelope canvases have a double number such as 10/20 to refer to a 10-mesh canvas. There are also two types of penelope canvas. One has evenly spaced double mesh that look the same and are evenly spaced up and down and from side to side. This is usually the best one to use. In the other type, there is a double thread running horizontally, or from side to side, and a twisted double thread running vertically, or up and down. This type is generally used as if it were a mono canvas.

Canvas comes on rolls and is cut from the roll, like fabric, when you buy it. The side edges are more tightly woven than the rest of the canvas and they are called selvedges. You'll find that the canvas is stiff, because it has been treated with sizing to make it appear to be evenly textured. The stiffness also adds body and keeps the spaces uniformly open.

Mono canvases are available in white and sometimes beige. They come in widths from 24 to 36 inches, although you can sometimes find wider canvas if you look hard. Penelope canvases are usually a shade of beige and often come in white in the larger mesh sizes. They come in widths from 24 to 40 inches and sometimes wider for the large-meshed types.

The size of the mesh determines the size of the stitches and therefore the names of the types of needlepoint. The smallest stitches done on fine canvases are called *petit point,* or "little stitch." These are delicate stitches done on canvases with 24 or more mesh to the inch and are mostly done by patient, experienced stitchers. You can use either mono or penelope canvas. The penelope canvas mesh can be pushed apart to form the smaller holes for petit point. The usual stitch size range is from 18 to 24 per inch.

Needlepoint, which is used as the name of a specific stitch as well as the general name, is done on mono or penelope canvas with from 10 to 16 mesh per inch. This is the most popular stitch, with the 10- and 12-mesh being the most widely used.

An effective idea for design details is to choose a 10/20-mesh penelope canvas and do most of the design in needlepoint and then separate the canvas mesh for the finer areas and do a petit point stitch, with 20 stitches to the inch for only those details. This type of combined stitching is very good for pictures and scenes where you need to do faces and other small sections.

Gros point, or "large stitch," is usually done on penelope canvas with 6 to 10 mesh per inch, although the name is sometimes used for finer canvases. It goes fairly quickly and is fun to do, since you can appreciate the results all the sooner.

Even faster, *quick point* is a relatively new idea, applied to stitches done on what is often referred to as rug canvases. These come in sizes from 3 to 5 mesh per inch and are always penelope canvas. If you plan to do a combined quick point and needlepoint—5- and 10-mesh stitching—be sure to buy the type of canvas which has evenly spaced double threads. The one with twisted vertical threads cannot be separated for the smaller stitches. Some of the rug type canvases come with a blue or red thread woven right into every few inches. These colored threads form a series of boxes on the canvas that make it easy to set up and plan a design.

For Bargello, mono canvas should always be used. The 10-, 12-, and 14-mesh canvases are the most popular for this work.

When you buy a canvas, of any size or type, be sure that it's a good quality net. The signs of a lesser quality canvas are bumps or knots in the woven threads, uneven spacing, uneven width of the threads themselves which will cause weak spots, and a dull finish. A good canvas will be smooth and slightly shiny, with a firm feeling to it. This will allow you to stitch easily without catching the yarn on rough spots or the canvas breaking down too much and becoming limp. For your first needlepoint stitches, buy a yard of 10-mesh mono canvas. This will be the best to practice on, since the mesh are quite easy to see and count. You'll have more than enough for your sampler and even for some projects.

Embroidery Backing Fabrics

When it comes to choosing backing fabrics for your embroidery, you'll find that the possibilities are almost endless. Virtually any kind of workable fabric can be used, since you regulate the size of the stitches by how you make them and the type of yarn or thread that you use.

The traditional crewel embroidery fabric is a natural-colored beige linen of the twill or regular weave. It is easily found in art needlework stores and large department stores in their craft sections. The weight and texture of this linen is widely favored by experienced embroiderers and its natural hue is suited to almost any design. Other fabrics of a similar weight, such as firm woolens, are also used for different effects. The main thing to look for is a compactly woven, well-bodied fabric.

For special types of work, such as cross stitch designs, the backing fabric should be woven so that it has an equal number of threads from side to side as it does from top to bottom. This is called an even weave and is essential if you have to count the threads to form the stitched pattern correctly. Even-weave linens and monk's cloth are among the often-used fabrics of this type.

Cotton fabrics in various weights are suited to many embroideries, but only the heavier weights will work for crewel. The stitcher who knows a bit about the craft will adapt it to application on almost any fabric, from velvet to burlap. These new fabric ideas offer a challenge that may be hard to resist. Stitchery is such a personal expression that you should use any-

Embroidery backing fabrics

thing that suits your own creativity. You can pick and choose with a little experimentation before starting the actual work to see which stitches and yarns seem just right for the backing you've decided on.

For the sampler, which should be your first project, buy a yard of linen intended for crewel embroidery. To learn the ins and outs of stitching, it can't be beaten. Later on, when you know the stitches and how they are done, you can be more flexible in your selection, as you'll have a sound stitch vocabulary based on the traditional fabric.

3

NEEDLES AND OTHER EQUIPMENT

The needles used for needlepoint and for embroidery are quite different and each is chosen to suit a specific task.

Needlepoint Needles

Needlepoint needles are generally called tapestry or yarn needles, and have blunt tips and large eyes that hold the yarn securely without being too hard to thread. The tips are blunt because the needle goes into the spaces in the canvas and never actually pierces the fabric as regular needles do. Needlepoint needles come in various sizes to suit the canvas, yarn, and type of work being done. The sizes run from number 13 to 24, with 13 being the heaviest weight with the largest eye and 24 being the lightest in weight with the smallest eye. The size 13 needle is used for quick point done on rug canvas, 24 for petit point on the finer canvases. (See the next chapter for information about the suitable needle, canvas, and yarn for all types of needlepoint stitching.) The needles usually come in packages of six, with the sizes 13, 16, 18, 20, and 22 being the easiest to find. You can buy a range of needle sizes fairly inexpensively.

To test a needle and see if it is the right one for the work you're doing, thread the needle. First, it should not crimp the yarn it's holding or seem impossible to thread. Then, when you try it out on the canvas, it should slip through easily without pushing the mesh apart at all. If it does push the mesh it is probably too large and a smaller one should be substituted.

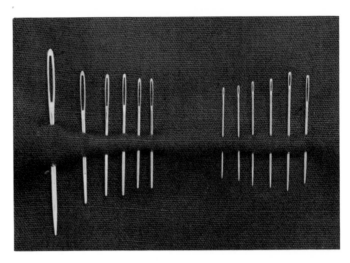

Needlepoint needles (left) and embroidery needles (right)

Embroidery Needles

Crewel and general embroidery needles have sharp points to stitch through the backing material easily, and fairly large eyes to accomodate the various yarns and threads. They are called embroidery sharps, crewel embroidery needles, and chenille needles for the larger sizes. The needles range in size from 1 to 10. The number 1 is the largest-eyed, heaviest needle, and number 10 is the smallest-eyed, lightest needle. Sizes 1 to 4 are considered large and are used with full strands of crewel and other wools and yarns. The medium-range sizes, from 4 to 7, are used with one strand of crewel wool, perle or pearl cotton, and with several strands of embroidery floss. Sizes 7 to 10 are the smallest, used for fine work with one or two strands of embroidery floss, silk, and other thin threads. (See the next chapter for a full description of the types of yarns and threads.)

You can buy the most widely used wool or yarn weight needle sizes in packages of six each. These are sizes 2, 3, and 4. The large, medium, and small groups of sizes can also be found in packages that contain a selection within the size range, usually fifteen or sixteen needles to the pack. It's always a good idea to have a range of sizes on hand, and these needles are also inexpensive.

To test your embroidery needles, use the thread and backing of your

24

project. Make a stitch and look at the base of the stitch, where the needle went into the fabric or came out of it. The yarn or thread should come out of the fabric in such a way that there are no open spaces around it. If the needle is too large, its very size will force too big an opening in the material and the yarn will not fill the opening well. Try out a smaller size until the yarn is neatly surrounded by the fabric where each stitch began or ended. If the needle is too small, you'll probably find it very difficult to thread and you should use a larger one that passes the test.

How to Thread a Needle

To thread a needle painlessly, there is a simple technique that can be used with either needlepoint or embroidery needles, as they both have large eyes. Hold the yarn in your left hand and the needle in your right. Fold the yarn around the needle and hold the folded yarn between your thumb and index finger. Tighten the yarn fold and move your fingers up so that the fold can just be seen between them as you look at your thumb and index finger. Slide the needle out, maintaining the fold with your other hand so that it looks the same as it did with the needle in place. Then

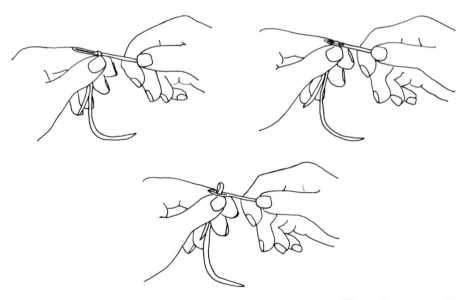

Threading a needle

25

carefully place the eye of the needle over the folded yarn. Keep holding the yarn fold in place and slide the needle in between your thumb and index finger. As the needle moves in between your fingers, the fold of yarn will slip into the eye, threading the needle. When the rounded end of the fold is through the eye, let go of it and catch it between your fingers on the other side, where it just came out, and pull it all the way through the eye so that the needle is threaded as usual. If you practice this method a couple of times, you'll have almost no difficulty threading any needle with a large eye. If you prefer an even simpler method, you can buy a needle threader, but it's not really necessary since this method works so well. If you're left-handed, reverse the hand positions to follow the same procedure.

Needle Storage

When you're not stitching, you should keep your needles in a safe place so that they're not lost, or dulled, in the case of embroidery needles. You can stick them into a pin cushion, which you can make yourself, or into a medium-sized cork. You can also use a small plastic container with a secure top. Just be sure that you know where they are. Unless you're only putting your work down for a brief moment, never stick the needles in the canvas or material. They just don't seem to stay put when left this way for more than a few minutes.

Scissors

Two pairs of scissors are helpful for doing needlepoint and embroidery. The first is a regular, large-fabric scissors, to cut the canvas or other backing to the correct size when you begin a project. The other is a small pair of embroidery scissors. These have sharp points on small blades and are used to snip the yarn or thread, and are invaluable for taking out stitches when necessary.

To keep scissors sharp, you should store them carefully and never use them to cut anything but fabric or thread. Never keep them in a work-basket with your other materials, for you can cut yourself too easily when reaching into it. A neat cover or case for your scissors is another interesting project you may want to do.

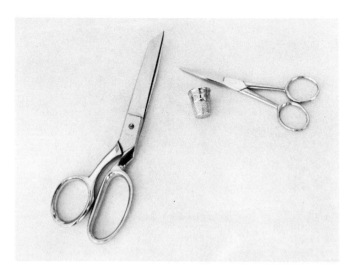

Scissors and a thimble

Thimbles

Many accomplished needleworkers wouldn't make a stitch without their thimbles. Although a thimble may seem awkward at first, it can be quite useful to protect your middle finger, particularly when you're working for a long time or on a fabric where you have to give the needle a little push each time you do a stitch. Thimbles should fit so that they are comfortably snug without being tight. If they're too loose, they're hard to work with. They come in many sizes, so try them out and get the right one. If using a thimble seems really difficult to you, you don't have to use one.

Hoops and Frames

A hoop or a frame is a must for doing embroidery, and many people feel that they're a boon to needlepoint, although not essential to it. They come in many sizes and styles.

The most basic hoop is a double circle made out of wood or metal, with one circle fitting tightly over and around the other. The smaller ring is placed under the backing fabric and the larger ring is placed on top. Then they are pushed together while the fabric is lightly stretched so that it becomes taut and easy to stitch. There are plain hoops, suitable for a small

27

Embroidery hoops

range of fabric thicknesses, but the best kind to get is made of wood and has an adjustable screw on the outer rim of the hoop. The screw allows for various weights of material since it can be made tighter or looser to suit. Hoops come in sizes, with a diameter of from 3 to 23 inches. The 10-inch or 12-inch is the most widely used size. They aren't expensive and you can start with one of these and be reasonably well-equipped for most stitching tasks. When you work with this type of hoop, you hold it in one hand and stitch with the other. For that reason, many prefer a standing hoop.

Standing hoops come in three different models. One has a clamp that is fastened onto the edge of a table so that you can sit in a chair at the table and be free to use both hands. Another true standing hoop has a short-legged base that sits on a table or on your lap. It can seem a bit less steady than the clamp type. The full-height standing hoop has a long-legged base that stands on the floor so that the hoop itself is at working height when you're sitting down. Although these hoops are quite useful, they're also quite expensive, so you shouldn't buy one until you've done a lot of stitching. Then you may certainly find it worthwhile because they do make certain types of work seem easier to do.

Sometimes, hoops are used for needlepoint as well as for embroidery, but they can stretch the mesh out of line where they close around the canvas. Hoops can be used for projects where the entire working area falls inside the hoop so that it doesn't matter if the outer edges are stretched a bit. When the work must be moved within the hoop, the finished needlepoint stitches can be crushed, so the smaller hoops are not advised for needlepoint.

Another type of stretching device used for both needlepoint and embroidery, although again more for embroidery, is a frame. The frames specifically made for the purpose are adjustable in both length and width, since they come with pegs and clamps on each corner. Frames come in both standing and lap-held models, which can be leaned against a table, with the other edge in your lap. Frames are also expensive, but they are practically indispensable for large embroidery projects where a hoop would have to be moved several times to cover the whole area to be stitched and might disturb the finished stitches.

To provide a frame with less expense, you can adapt an old picture frame, as long as it's sturdy enough to hold the fabric without buckling or warping. Just check the frame and remove any tacks or other attachments originally meant to secure the picture into the frame. You can sew the project into the frame. If there are rough wooden edges, smooth them with sandpaper so that they don't catch the canvas, fabric, or threads. Another frame that you can use is sold in art supply stores. This is called a stretcher frame, used for mounting artists' canvases for oil paints. You buy the frame in two sets of slats, one double set for the sides and one for the top and bottom. This way, you can choose the size you want for each. The

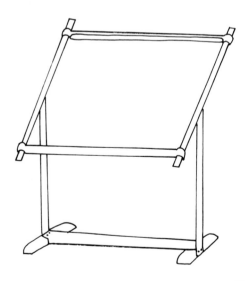

Left: Embroidery frame

Below: Stretcher frame

slats are then fitted together at the corners with the notches built into the ends for this purpose.

Blocking Equipment

When you finish a piece of needlepoint, and sometimes an embroidery, the stitches may have pulled it out of its original shape. To remedy this you block it, or re-form it into the original shape, using water and an iron on a board. For this procedure, you'll need a fairly large sheet of plywood or other sturdy compressed board that you can stick pins into and that is generally larger than the projects you make. You'll also need some rust-proof pins or tacks to hold the work in place while blocking.

Other Equipment

Other equipment that you'll need can often be found around the house. A ruler, tape measure, or other measuring device is an essential. For needlepoint, you'll also need felt tip marking pens that are truly water-proof, to mark the design on the canvas, and masking tape to bind the raw, cut edges of the canvas before you start to stitch so that it doesn't unravel or catch the yarn. For embroidery, transfer pencils, dressmaker's chalk, or carbon paper can be used to mark the design on the fabric.

4

YARNS, THREADS, AND FIBERS

The yarns, threads, and fibers of needlepoint and embroidery are doubtless one of stitchery's greatest assets. Their textures, colors, and appealing qualities are a pleasure in themselves. When you can, go to a needlecraft supply store that has a really wide variety of yarns on sale. Then, you'll be able to see just what is available and get the ones you want.

The type of work you're doing naturally influences the kinds of yarn or thread that you buy. In needlepoint, the open spaces of the canvas are pretty demanding, so that you must get the type of yarn that fits the canvas you want to use. In crewel embroidery, there is a special yarn called crewel yarn that usually gives the best results, since it is made for this purpose. However, general embroidery can be done with almost any type of yarn or thread, according to your own inspiration.

The most widely used fiber in stitchery is wool. Recently synthetic or man-made yarns have been used, but the natural beauty and luster of wool maintains its position as the favorite. Make sure that any wool yarn you buy is mothproof, colorfast, and preshrunk. Synthetics usually have these qualities as part of their appeal. Cotton is used a lot in embroidery, and those willing to pay its fairly steep price use silk. Metallics and other unusual or exotic blends can be used in embroidery and for needlepoint with patience and pretesting to see whether they'll work out.

As you look at a piece of yarn, you'll see that it is made up of separate little strands twisted together that are called ply. The number of ply in a piece of yarn is often used to give it a name, such as 3-ply yarn. If you twist yarn in the other direction than the twist goes, you can see the individual ply that make it up.

Needlepoint Yarns and Requirements

Two types of yarn are most often used for needlepoint. They are called Persian and tapestry yarns. The Persian wool is made up of three plies that are easily separated for use when a thinner yarn is needed. You can use one, two, or all three plies of this yarn. Tapestry yarn is a bit heavier than Persian, being made of four plies that cannot be separated and are always used as is. For the larger-mesh canvases, a type of yarn used for knitting called worsted is sometimes used, but it is not as strong or attractive in a finished work as needlepoint's more usual yarns. Another popular yarn is rug yarn, used on the large-mesh canvases with good results. It's available in both wool and synthetics.

In needlepoint, you want the yarn to cover the canvas well without being too thick so that it pushes the mesh apart. In Bargello this is particularly important because the canvas shows through quite easily when too thin a yarn is used. To test the yarn before you begin any project in needlepoint, it's a good idea to make a sample swatch, using the identical needle, canvas, yarn, and stitch of the project. Then, you can make any needed adjustments before you've gone too far, trying them out on the sample piece. As a general guideline, on the rug-weight canvases, from 3 to 5 mesh per inch, you'll use a size 13 needle, with one strand of rug yarn; on a 10-mesh canvas, you'll use a size 16 or 18 needle with a full 3-ply strand of Persian yarn or one strand of tapestry yarn; on a 12- or 14-mesh canvas, you'll use a size 18 or 20 needle with two strands of Persian yarn (or one strand of tapestry yarn if it is for Bargello only—it won't fit in needlepoint); and for petit point canvases, you'll use a 22 or 24 needle with a single strand of Persian yarn. Since this is open to variation due to the stitch used and so on, you can change the supplies you're using to suit the work as shown by the sample.

For accent, or on their own on the smaller mesh canvases for special projects, you can use embroidery threads like pearl or perle cotton or six-strand embroidery floss, as long as you test them first. Threads with a greater shine, like the metallics, can also be used for accent in small areas on articles that won't receive a lot of wear.

Left: Needlepoint and embroidery yarns and threads. Right: Persian and embroidery yarns, cut into convenient lengths for stitching and tied in the middle so they don't become tangled.

Crewel and Embroidery Threads

As mentioned above, cotton thread used for embroidery is known as perle or pearl cotton, which has a twisted appearance with a fine sheen to it. Six-strand embroidery floss is also made out of cotton and can be divided for finer work. These threads are most often used on cotton or linen fabrics. When a fine thread like silk is used, its backing should be of equal quality, so silk fabric or velvet is the best.

Crewel yarn is used for crewel work on linen and fine woolens. It is very much like the Persian yarn used for needlepoint except that it often comes in 2-ply instead of three. Further experimentation may lead you to use rug or knitting weight wools or other yarns with interesting textures.

Novelty yarns and fibers, with an incredible variety of colors and textures, are also open to exploration. In embroidery you can be flexible, open to new materials, lending a completely individual quality to your work. It's really up to you. Just try them out and see what you like best.

In general, for the heavy weight yarns on heavy fabrics, like woolens, you'll use a number 2 needle. For crewel yarn on linen or lighter woolens,

33

a number 3 or 4 needle will be best. For a full six strands of embroidery floss, on linen or other fabrics, you'll use a size 5 or 6 needle. The same sizes are suitable for pearl cotton, which is used one strand at a time, since it can't be separated. For three or less strands of floss on light fabrics, you'll use a size 7 or 8 needle. Here again, making a sample using the same needle, fabric, thread, and stitch of the project will be invaluable to you in checking the work before you begin the actual project.

Buying Yarn

Yarn for needlepoint and crewel comes in a variety of ways. The most usual is a ready-wound ball that has a pull-out center strand for easy yarn flow. The center strand is usually quite visible, coming out of the side edge of the ball and going down under the label that is found around the yarn. This is the best way to unroll the yarn, as the outer strand never unrolls as easily. The other way these yarns are often sold is in a hank, or loose circle of strands. To use a hank of yarn, you carefully unfold it so that you can see the circle of strands. Then, you flatten the circle out and cut right through each end, so that you have two large bunches of cut strands. These strands are the best way to work, because in needlepoint and crewel you can't use too long a length of yarn while stitching or it wears out from being pulled through the canvas or fabric. Once you've cut the yarn, tie a loose knot in the center of the cut strands so that the yarn doesn't get tangled up in itself. Crewel yarn is also sold on cards, with several long strands wound around a piece of cardboard. These can be good to use when you only want a small amount of each color.

The skeins and hanks of yarn come in lengths, from 25 to 40 yards each. This is important because yarns are dyed in a complex process that does not always produce an identical shade. Therefore, you should try to buy enough yarn to complete an entire project at once, so that you can be sure that the colors will match precisely. The batches of yarn are dyed in what are called dye lots, and each ball or skein will have a number or letter combination, indicating which dye lot it came from. Even when buying a lot of yarn at once, you should check the dye lot to be sure that all your yarn came from the same one.

To estimate how much yarn you'll need in needlepoint, work a square inch of the stitch you plan to use on the same size canvas you will use. Since you probably won't have the same yarn on hand, you can use any yarn of the same weight, and preferably from the same manufacturer, for the test. Then, take the measurements of your project and multiply the width by the height, to find out how many square inches there are of canvas to be covered in the project. Then, multiply the amount of yarn it took to do the inch square to find out how many yards of yarn you'll need. If the measurement of yarn to do the square was in inches, be sure to divide the final total by twelve, to the find the number of feet, and then again by three to find the number of yards. The total will be for all of the colors in your design, so you should then figure out approximately how much of the design each color covers. Extra yarn can always be used in other projects, so you don't have to be too exact. As an example, the most widely used stitch is probably the continental stitch. If this stitch is done on 10-mesh canvas, it uses about one and one-half yards of tapestry yarn to a square inch. If your design is 12″ by 12″, its total in square inches is 144. Then, you multiply 1.5 by 144 for a total of 180 yards of yarn. If you're using 40-yard balls, this comes to 4.5 skeins. Therefore, you'd buy five skeins or balls of yarn for this project.

You'll find that as you work, you'll come to know the requirements and will be able to guess fairly accurately how much yarn you'll need for a given project. Another possibility, if you're in a good needlework store, is to talk to the salesperson, who will probably be able to tell you just how much yarn to buy by looking at the size of the project and knowing which stitch you plan to use. In any case, leftover yarn always comes in handy. You'll find that many design ideas call for small amounts of various colors.

For your first needlepoint sampler, if you have a 10-mesh canvas, you can buy either tapestry or Persian yarn and use the colors you prefer. If you can find imported yarn, it often comes in small amounts, of about 10 yards per skein, so that you can get several colors to experiment with.

For crewel and other embroideries, you'll usually need a lot less yarn than you would for a similar size piece of needlepoint. If you can find the smaller amounts of crewel yarn, on cards, you can buy a few for your first sampler. For embroidery, the floss comes in pull-out skeins and is very inexpensive, so that you can buy several different colors to start out with.

To make buying supplies a good experience, try to find a needlework store with a wide range of materials so that you'll be able to see easily just what is available. While you're there, you may see kits, containing everything you need to make a needlepoint or crewel work, except the hoop in the latter type of stitchery. The kits come with enough yarn, a printed canvas or fabric and a needle, so that you simply fill in the outlined backing with the materials provided, according to the written instructions that come with the kits. Although this is not the most imaginative way to work, you might find that it is an easy way to learn the stitches. In needlepoint, there are also imported canvases with the central design completely worked; you buy the wool needed and fill in the background. These will give you a lesson in how to do the basic stitch and fill in around a design motif, but many people find that working in only one background color offers little creative challenge. Another type of preconceived crewel design is an iron-on transfer, or design outline. These are a bit more interesting than the kits because you choose the stitches and colors to fill in the outlines yourself, rather than following an entire packaged idea.

While you're looking, see if there are any odd lots, or ends of production groups of yarn, on sale. These can be a real bargain and may contain just the colors you want.

If you don't live near a needlework supply store, there are several excellent mail order suppliers (see page 156) that will send you a catalogue, often free of charge, with photographs and written descriptions of everything you will need. The added attraction here is that many large companies will give you a discount on orders of, for example, twelve skeins of yarn or more, allowing mixed colors, that can be a real saving. Also, the per item prices of mail order suppliers are often lower than those in stores.

5

PATTERNS AND PROCEDURES

Choosing a design for stitchery is an exciting experience. It's completely up to you, so that you can explore many areas and find so many design suggestions that you'll never run out of new ideas that you'll want to try. The most rewarding designs to use are the products of your own creativity —drawings, paintings, sketches, even doodles are remarkably effective when done in stitches. The very texture and colors of the stitches add a new feeling to your work. Look at things you've already done or make some new drawings or paintings. Just get some paper and colored pencils, pens, crayons, or paints, and let your imagination take over. Cutouts and other paper constructions are also good inspirations for needlework.

For other ideas that might suggest stitcheries to you, look at magazines, books, photographs, and other pictures for flowers, animals, scenes, interesting patterns, and geometrics. Then adapt these things in your own way. The most basic line drawings are well suited to stitched work, using simple shapes and forms. The beauty of needlework is the freedom with which you can choose designs and patterns. Even a large single flower placed in a bright background makes an attractive stitched work. Once you begin you'll have trouble just finding the time to work out all of the ideas that come to you.

When it comes to color, let your own preferences be your guide. At first, it may be easiest to work with a few colors on a fairly neutral background, until you gain a firsthand knowledge of how color works in the type of stitchery you're doing.

Design ideas

39

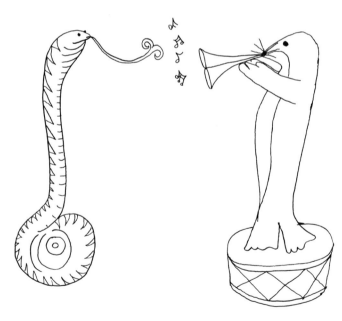

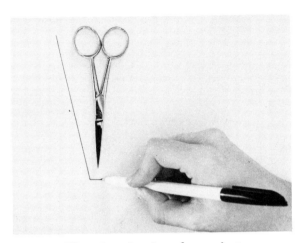

Planning the size of a project

Planning the Size of a Project

When you are making something for a specific purpose, the best way to plan it is to make a paper pattern. For example, if you want to make a scissors case, trace the shape of the scissors onto a piece of paper. Then, to plan the case itself, add an inch all around to allow for seams and folds. In needlepoint, the canvas naturally shrinks a bit after it's stitched, so that you need to add an additional amount to each edge to allow for the smaller finished size. On small projects, add between ½ and ¾ of an inch. On larger projects, over 12″ by 12″, add from ¾ to one inch. Even if you have a larger stitched area than you actually need, it will be quite useful in making up the article, since you must sew any seams or other finishing methods within the stitched area. Embroidery also shrinks the backing to an extent, but much less, so that you can add only between ¼ and ½ an inch. In each case, the working canvas or fabric is cut out in a square or a rectangle, not in the actual shape of the article, which is cut out when finished.

Needlepoint Margins

In needlepoint, you also need to leave an unstitched area of plain canvas around the worked section. This margin should be at least 1½ to 2 inches on all sides, or in other words, a full 3 or 4 inches of unworked canvas up and down and from side to side. This area is needed later on to finish the work correctly, so you should make sure you add it at the beginning. Another reason it will be helpful to you is that sometimes the canvas shrinks even more than expected and when you start to make up the article you realize that you need to add an extra row or two of stitches. With a good margin all around, you'll be able to do it without problems. Once the article is made up, you can always cut off the excess canvas if it seems too bulky. While you work, remember to cover the raw canvas edges with masking tape.

Embroidery Margins

In other forms of stitchery you also leave a margin of unworked material of 3 inches or more around the area that will be stitched. Remember that this is in addition to the seam allowance used to make up the article. If you plan to cover the material with stitches, add another ½ inch for the natural shrinkage that will occur. When you've cut out the fabric, fold under the rough edges and baste them in place, by hand or machine, so that they don't unravel while stitching. Later on, you can undo the basted edges if you need the excess fabric for seams or to otherwise mount the stitchery.

Design Enlargement

Once you've planned the size of your project and its stitched area, you may find that the design you've chosen must be made larger to fit your plans. If you're using a drawing of your own, draw the outlines of the project's stitched area on a sheet of paper and then redraw the picture inside those outlines so that the size looks right for the project.

For a more complex enlarging job, you can use a ruler for the squares method. To do this, draw a square or rectangular outline around the small design, whichever fits better. Then draw a square or rectangle, depending on which you chose for the small design, in the size that you want the larger version to be. Measure off two sides of the small design, making dots so that each of the sides is broken up into equally spaced sections. Then, following the measured spaces, draw straight lines right across the small design so that they reach the opposite edge in the same spot. Then do the same thing on the next side so that the entire design is covered with a series of boxes, formed by the crossing lines. On the larger outline, measure off the same number of spaces and draw the boxes in the same way. As this outline is larger in the first place, when you draw an equal number of boxes, each box itself will be larger than the corresponding box on the small design. An easy way to do this is to use even measurements, such as ½ inch on the small design and 1 inch on the large one. To enlarge even more, use 2-inch boxes on the larger version. Whichever you choose, always be sure that the number of boxes on each is the same.

To do the actual enlarging, you follow the grid, as the boxes are called, and copy the part of the design that is contained in each smaller box into the corresponding larger box. If you place the large and small versions side by side and copy each section of the design as found in each box carefully, when you're finished, you'll have a copy of the smaller design that is just the size you need. This also works in reverse to make a design smaller, by using an equal number of smaller boxes and following the same procedure. You can also have a design change in shape to some extent as long as the same number of boxes are followed in each version you plan.

Another method of design enlargement is to take the design to a photographic store and have a photostat made. They can make it any size you want in both the positive—white background with black lines—and negative—black background with white lines. The positive version is usually the most useful. However, you should have no trouble with the squares method once you've tried it, and you should use that one whenever possible.

Needlepoint Design Transfer

When you have the enlarged or drawn design in the size you want, you transfer it onto the needlepoint canvas so that you can follow it while stitching. To do this you'll need a fine-tipped waterproof marking pen and the canvas. Be sure that the marker is really waterproof by cutting off a

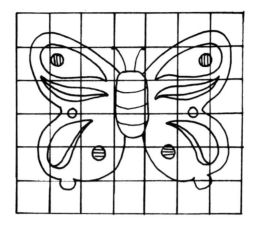

Enlarging a design with the squares method

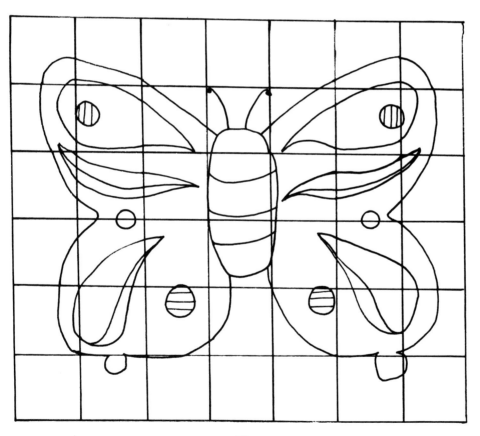

45

small section of canvas, marking a line or two on it and dipping it in water. If it runs at all, don't use that pen or you'll ruin your canvas. The really waterproof kind are found in art supply stores. Buy one in black and one in a medium shade, like gray or blue. The black color may show through if you're using light colored yarns. Use the medium marker for light colored projects.

To prepare the canvas, mark the boundaries of the stitched area with a ruler. Then mark the exact center of each side. Holding the ruler at the side marks, find the center of the canvas and put a faint mark there. If you haven't already done so, put masking tape around the raw edges of the canvas. Then measure and mark the center of the design and place the canvas on top of it, using the center marks to line it up perfectly. Use the marker to copy all of the design outlines directly onto the canvas. If there are many parts, copy the heavy outlines first, adding the smaller details when you've finished the larger ones. If you have trouble seeing the design through the canvas, hold it up to a window and let the sun shine through it. Or, if there is a glass-topped table that you can use, put a lamp under it and place the design and canvas on the table so that the light shines through it. Either way, you'll be able to see all of the outlines clearly.

When you've finished tracing the design, you can color it if you like—in

Transferring a design onto a needlepoint canvas

colors representing the yarn colors—to make it easier to follow while stitching. For Bargello canvases, you don't need to mark the design, but they are often lightly colored so that the stitches blend nicely with the canvas.

To make the work easier to block, or put into shape, later on, mark its outlines on a sheet of wrapping paper before you color the canvas. Draw the entire outline on the paper and use a ruler to mark the exact centers of the sides on the paper. This will be a helpful guide for blocking it after it is stitched.

The best thing to use to color the canvas is acrylic paints. They look like oil paints, but can be washed off the brushes and your hands with plain soap and water. When they dry, they're not affected by water any longer. They come in bright colors that are easy to mix so that you can buy a basic set and blend the shades you need using water or the medium, as it's called, that you can buy to go with the paints.

To color the canvas, thin the paints with as little water as possible, or use the medium. Be sure that they're thin enough to color the canvas without filling up the spaces in it, which would make it impossible to stitch. Then, fill in the design outlines on the canvas with a paint brush, working slowly and carefully. Let the canvas dry for a day before stitching.

If you don't want to color the canvas, you can make a colored version on paper and follow it as you stitch. If you're using different stitches within the work, you can also write their names on the paper pattern in the appropriate areas. Another way to show where the colors are to go is to make a loose stitch of each color with the yarn of the project within the correct outline of the design.

Needlepoint Charts

Charts are often used to plan a needlepoint design. When you use a chart, the canvas isn't marked at all, except for the outlines of the stitched area itself. Drawing central marks is also helpful, but not essential. Charts are always used for Bargello, where the first line of stitching is often enough to show how the entire design will work.

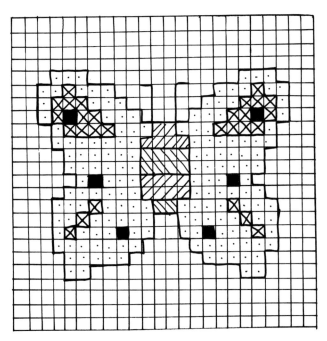

A needlepoint chart

Charts are made on graph paper, which is divided into many squares that stand for the mesh of the canvas. Each square on the canvas is shown by a square on the chart. The stitches themselves are shown by dots, lines, X's or other symbols, depending on how complex the design is. When there is more than one color, each is shown by a symbol and the name of the color and the symbol are shown in a box at the bottom of the chart. If there is one background color that is used a lot, it is often shown by blank squares. Otherwise, the blanks stand for a color in the design, as shown in the box.

To follow a chart, you set up the canvas, marking the outlines and the center if you wish, making sure that there are the same number of mesh outlined as there are boxes in the chart. Remember that the squares on the chart stand for stitches, which are made over a mesh or intersection in the canvas, so that you count the mesh and not the spaces. If you have trouble keeping track as you count, count the mesh on the outside of the outline and mark a dot on each tenth mesh. Then, if you lose track, you won't have to recount from the beginning.

If you are following a chart, read any instructions that came with it carefully, since they can sometimes be confusing. This occurs when the charts are made for the more complex stitches, where one stitch or stitch unit may cover more than a single mesh. In this type of chart, each box may stand for one whole stitch, no matter how large it is. In other charts for the same stitch, the stitch is drawn as it appears on the canvas when finished, including the number of mesh it actually covers. However, this will be indicated if you read the accompanying information.

To work a design from any type of chart, you generally start with the motifs, as you do in any needlepoint design. This means that you stitch the smaller parts of the design first, then the larger ones, and finally the background. That's why the center mark can be useful. It helps you to figure out just where each motif is placed. The first few stitches are usually the most difficult to place, with the following ones being done more easily around them. As long as you count accurately, you should have no problems. If you're doing an overall pattern where there are no main sections, or one that would be very hard to count out, start in the upper right-hand corner. If you're left-handed, it may be better to start in the upper left or lower left-hand corner instead. After the first stitches, part of the pattern will be established and it will be easier to work. To keep track of just where you are on the chart, cross out a line or group of stitches on the chart with a see-through color pencil when you finish that section. Then you'll know where you stopped whenever you start to stitch the next area.

Embroidery Design Transfer

Embroidery designs are also marked on the backing before stitching. There are a few ways to do it. The easiest is to use a special pen or pencil that you can buy in needlework supply stores called a transfer pencil. They come in light and dark, the light one for use on dark fabrics and the dark one for use on light fabrics. To use a transfer pencil, first copy your design onto tracing or other lightweight paper that you can see through. Take the transfer pencil and copy the outlines of the design on the back or wrong side of the paper, just as you see them when the paper is turned face down. Then, take the fabric you are using and place the paper face up on

Transferring a design onto an embroidery fabric

it, with the wrong side of the paper touching the right side of the fabric, which should be face up. Pin the corners of the design, outside of the area to be stitched, so that it doesn't slip around while transferring. Then, carefully place the fabric and design on an ironing board. Set an iron between warm and hot—don't use steam if it's a steam iron—and place the iron on the transfer. Lift it up and set it down in the next spot, rather than sliding it as you would when actually ironing something. Make sure that you've covered the entire design; unpin a corner and check to see that the transfer has taken place. If not, re-pin and iron the transfer again until the design is clearly visible. Remove the design by unpinning it and lifting it off the fabric. There's your transferred design, ready for stitching.

The reason that you trace the design on the wrong side of the tracing paper is so that the tracing will be reversed, like the image in a mirror, and appear correctly when it's ironed onto the fabric. If you plan the design to go one way and then use the transfer pencil on the right side, when the design is on the fabric it will be reversed. If your design is symmetrical—

with both sides the same—it won't matter if it's reversed and you can draw over the outlines with the transfer pencil on the right side of the design without tracing it first. To check this, hold your design up to a mirror. If it looks the same, you can use the right side.

Another method of transferring an embroidery design is to use good quality carbon paper. You'll also need some tracing paper, straight pins, and an empty ball-point pen or a knitting needle. Make a copy of the design on tracing paper. Place the fabric to be stitched on a hard surface, place a sheet of carbon paper, with the carbon side touching the fabric, on the planned design area. Put the traced design onto the carbon paper, face up. Pin the corners to be sure they don't slip. Then use the empty ball-point pen or knitting needle to go over all of the design outlines, pressing hard. Then unpin and lift a corner to see whether it's dark enough to see each outline clearly. If not, go over them again. When you have a clear, well-defined design, unpin the design and remove it and the carbon paper. If you're using a lot of light colors, the transfer pencil may be better, since the carbon might come off on very light colored yarns. In the carbon paper method, the design goes onto the fabric as you see it so that you can work on the right side. You should make a tracing, since the design might be ruined while going over the outlines and you should keep the original on hand to check with while stitching.

Dressmaker's chalk is also used for design transfer in embroidery. It comes in pencil form or in small rectangular pieces. There are several colors and you can use it to draw right on the fabric because you can rub it off if you make a mistake. It is good for simple designs that can be copied while drawing, without having to be as accurate as the other methods. One drawback is that it does come off and you may have to refresh the design outlines in the middle of stitching it.

Embroidery patterns are not colored in on the fabric. The best way to follow the colors is to paint, pencil, or crayon them onto your original paper design. You can cut snips of the yarn or thread and tape them onto a corner of the paper with the color of paint or pencil you used for that color right next to it. Then you can keep the paper design with your stitching and use it as a guide while you work.

51

Blocking Needlepoint

When you finish a piece of needlepoint, you may notice that it has been pulled out of shape by the stitches. This always happens to varying degrees, depending on which stitch you've used. It's not hard to return it to the correct shape with the right equipment. You'll need a large sheet of plywood or sturdy pressed board, the brown wrapping paper outline you made before (as described in the beginning of this chapter), a towel or sponge, an iron, and lots of waterproof push pins or tacks. Tack or tape the brown paper outline onto the board. When placing the needlepoint for blocking, you usually put it face up, so that you can see it, and the stitches remain textured and slightly puffy. If you want a flatter, smooth surface on the stitches, place the needlepoint face down. Whichever you do, the rest of the procedure is the same.

To prepare the needlepoint for blocking, check its appearance. If it looks clean but warped, use a sponge or towel and cold water and dampen the wrong side of the stitches. If it's soiled, use a sponge dipped in lukewarm soapy water and carefully wash the right side. Use the kind of soap made for fine woolens. Then use clear water and rinse out the sponge and then rinse out the needlepoint by going over it with the sponge until you're sure that all the soap has been removed.

The canvas is now ready to be blocked. Place it on the outlined wrapping paper. If the needlepoint looks smaller than the outline, it is due to the natural shrinkage that takes place. As you follow the paper outline, which has not shrunk, it will be a bit larger than the actual stitching in many cases. Line up the needlepoint and one corner of the outline and put in a pin or tack in the unstitched area. Move to the opposite corner. Hold the tacked corner in place with one hand and stretch the opposite corner with the other hand until it gets as close to the outline as possible. Let go of the first corner and put in a tack in the second corner. Do the next two corners the same way. Then, put tacks or pins into the edges, working in the unstitched area, placing a pin every inch or so to hold the needlepoint firmly in place. Match the edges to the paper outline as nearly as possible. When you're finished, there are two ways to proceed. The first is to cover the needlepoint with a towel that has been wet and thoroughly wrung out.

Blocking needlepoint

Then take an iron, with the setting on wool, and iron over the towel. The steam that is created by the wet towel blocks the piece. Then remove the towel and let the needlepoint dry for at least a day, or until bone dry. If you've washed or thoroughly dampened the needlepoint, you can use a second method, which is merely to let it dry for as long as it takes to be completely dry.

In almost all cases, your needlepoint is now ready to be assembled or otherwise mounted. If you've used a stitch that warps the canvas badly, you may have to block it once or twice more. All but the most badly warped canvases will eventually come out straight, with a bit of patience.

Blocking Embroidery

The procedure for blocking a finished piece of embroidery is dictated by the condition of the work. Compare it to your design and see whether it is warped at all. Often it won't be, since embroidery is worked in a hoop and few of the stitches slant in the way that needlepoint stitches do. Also check to see whether it has been soiled from being handled.

If the stitchery is clean and the outlines match the design outlines closely, you can just iron it and it will be ready for mounting or assembly. To iron embroidery, pad the ironing board by putting a couple of folded towels on it, so that you have a nice soft surface and the stitches don't get flattened out by the iron. Place the embroidery on the padded surface face down. If you have a steam iron, set it at warm or wool and steam. Carefully iron the wrong side until it's unwrinkled. If you have a regular iron, wet a towel or pressing cloth and wring it out. Place it on the face-down embroidery, being sure that the embroidery has no wrinkles in it, or they'll be pressed in. Then set the iron on warm to hot and press over the damp cloth. In both cases, the steam created by the iron, or the wet cloth and iron, presses the fabric backing so that it's nice and smooth and fluffs up the stitches so that they look their best.

If the embroidery is pulled out of shape somewhat but is clean, you block it. You'll need a large plywood or other board, a brown wrapping paper outline of the original design outlines, rustproof push pins or tacks, a bowl of lukewarm water, and a sponge. In blocking embroidery, you pin it to the board and then wet it. First, pin the paper outline on the board. Then line up the embroidery as well as you can. Always block embroidery face up so that the stitches aren't flattened. The texture and slightly raised quality will be lost if blocked face down. Start to tack the embroidery down in one corner, working near the edge within the folded extra margin. Put in a pin or tack about every inch, working along the edge until you reach the next corner, lightly pulling on the fabric to be sure that it is smooth and taut. Pull the fabric with the grain, that is, from side to side or up and down, not on the bias, which would be from opposite corners. A bias pull will make the fabric even more distorted than it was when you began to block it. After you have one whole edge tacked, move to the opposite side. If you did the top, do the bottom, and if you did one side, do the other. Pulling lightly to smooth it out, tack the next edge. Then do the two remaining sides. Doing opposite sides makes it easier to flatten the fabric without distorting it. Then dip the sponge in the water and squeeze out the excess. Starting in the center of the stitching, wet the entire em-

Blocking embroidery

broidery with the sponge. Be sure that all of the stitching and all of the fabric are completely wet, without any dry spots. Leave it to dry, away from heat or bright lights, for at least a day, or until thoroughly dry. If you don't assemble or mount it right away, you can store it by rolling it around itself or a cardboard cylinder, like an empty roll of wrapping paper, with the stitches facing out. If the stitches face in, they'll be cramped together. Embroidery should never be folded, and rolling it will keep it fresh until you mount it.

If the embroidery is soiled, which will occur from the handling needed to do the stitches, you can wash it carefully and then block it. Use a good soap, intended for woolens and fine fabrics, and cool to lukewarm water. Place the piece in the soapy water and just swish the water through it, without rubbing or stretching the fabric. Then take it out right away, without letting it soak, as might be recommended for other fabrics on the box of soap. Rinse it carefully in plenty of cool water until the water runs clear and you are sure that all the soap is out. Then place it flat on a towel and roll it up to get out the excess moisture. Never wring it. Unroll the towel and smooth it out. Let the embroidery dry for a while until it's damp but not really wet. You can then block it according to the directions just given by pinning it to the board. Since it is already damp, you don't need to dampen it again when you've finished pinning it down; just leave it until completely dry. While pinning a fabric that has been washed, you'll find that you don't need to pull it very much because the damp fabric stretches more than the dry fabric would.

Finishing Techniques

The blocked, dry needlepoint or embroidery is now ready to be mounted, assembled, or otherwise put into its final form. The finishing techniques are employed depending on what you are making and how it is put together.

Finishing Needlepoint

Blocked needlepoint is made up into the finished article according to general rules that you can follow for almost all pieces. For the most complex items, such as upholstery, leather-soled slippers, pocketbooks with more than a simple shape, or luggage, you'll need to have them mounted by a professional, experienced in this kind of work. However, any one of these jobs will be very expensive and usually requires a specific type of pattern so that you should always check it out before you do even the first stitch. Smaller articles, such as pillows, can also be professionally mounted, but you can do them yourself and there's no need to go to a professional.

One of the basic methods for finishing an article is to sew seams to assemble the final form of the project. The extra canvas margin that you left around the stitched area is used as a seam allowance when assembling an article. In most cases, you'll have more than you need when you have finished blocking, so that you cut off the masking tape and the canvas beneath it, leaving a ¾ inch margin or seam allowance all the way around the stitched area. This is still a bit large for a seam, but if it's too bulky you can always trim it when the seam is complete, and it's easier to work this way. To sew the parts of an item with two or more seam edges together, you can use a sewing machine or hand sewing. A machine is fine if you have one and are used to operating it, but in most cases it will be easiest and best to sew the seams by hand.

To keep the seam from unraveling while you sew, get some white liquid glue that dries clear. Put a thin line of the glue along the newly cut edge and allow it to dry completely. To sew, you'll need a fairly small tapestry needle and some strong thread in the color of the project.

To sew two stitched needlepoint pieces together, fold the bare canvas allowance to the wrong side on each section. The fold should be just inside the stitched area, in the first or second row. If you don't have enough stitched area to allow for this, you can add a row of stitches with the yarn of the project. Then baste the seam allowance to the backs of the stitches. Line up the two parts that will make up the seam so that they match exactly, stitch for stitch. Thread the needle with your sewing thread, double it and knot it. Slide the needle into the back of one folded edge and bring it to the front through the fold itself. Then, carefully sew from side to side, back and forth, matching up the stitches as you go, sewing one to the opposing stitch in the same place on the other side. Pull lightly on the thread so that the pieces come together and the seam doesn't show. Continue to the end of the seam, working into the stitches. Bring the needle through to the back and end off the thread. You can use this method to sew any two pieces of needlepoint together, even after they have been partially assembled. When you're done, if the seam allowance is too bulky to lie flat, cut it to ½ an inch. If the seam will receive wear, glue the raw edge with white glue, and allow to dry. Always be sure that you sew within a row or two of stitches, since the bare canvas by itself is not strong enough to hold a seam and will eventually come apart.

If you do want to use a sewing machine, place the right sides of the needlepoint together and pin the two pieces face to face. Use strong thread and set the machine on 8 to 10 stitches per inch, with a fairly light pressure to allow for the bulk of the two needlepointed sections to flow smoothly while stitching. Sew just inside the stitched area, one or two rows of stitches in from the raw canvas, and go slowly. If the seam will receive a lot of wear, sew another row of machine stitches right next to the first when you finish the seam. Then, trim the seam allowances to ½ inch and add glue if the back of the seam will be exposed in the completed article.

Needlepoint Pillows

Needlepoint pillows are one of the most popular projects. They're bright and cheerful and you can't have too many. They're also quite easy to put together. Whenever you sew a needlepoint seam, joining the needlepoint to another fabric as you do in pillows, you place the right sides of the needlepoint and the fabric together to ready them for sewing. Good materials to use for this type of pillow backing are felt, corduroy, velvet, and—for a special touch—suede. You cut out the fabric so that it is the same size as the trimmed section of needlepoint. Pin the fabric to the needlepoint with the right sides facing in. Then, sew a seam just inside the stitched area, working from the side of the needlepoint so that you can see what's happening as you sew. If you're sewing by hand, use a regular sharp needle and strong thread and do the backstitch. If you're sewing by machine, follow the general instructions above. Sew around the pillow, including all four corners and only three sides, since you need to leave the last one open for stuffing. Turn the sewn pillow right side out. If you're using a pillow form, measure the size before you do the needlepoint itself so that it matches, and then after you've finished the seam, fold the form and slip it into the opening in the last side. If you're using shredded or loose stuffing, the pillow can be any shape, and you stuff it through the opening. The opening is then sewn closed by hand, working carefully from side to side as you sew so that the seam doesn't show.

When you finish sewing any seam in needlepoint, if there are any bare spots of canvas showing through, use the yarn of the project to carefully stitch over and cover them, using the same stitch as the needlepoint itself. If any seams are curves, before you turn them right side out, make small clips into the canvas at intervals with scissors so that the seam can spread out or close up as necessary to accommodate the curve.

Making a Lining for Needlepoint

Many articles that you can make in needlepoint must be lined, for long life. Just what kind of lining to use depends on the size and weight of the object. Clothing, such as vests, should be lined with taffeta or a similar lining fabric, found in the sewing department in stores. Belts, book covers, eyeglass cases, and other similar articles should be lined, and felt is the easiest to use because you can cut it to size without it unraveling. For a luxurious touch, leather or suede linings can be used, but they can be tricky to work with. For simple square or rectangular pocketbooks or tote bags that you can make up yourself, a nice heavy duty lining, such as cotton canvas or burlap, should be used. For further stiffness and strength, an additional inner lining that fits between the lining and the needlepoint is included. This is called an interlining and the heavier weight ones, such as buckram, are usually the best for things that need a definite shape.

To make a lining, you use the paper pattern for the article you've planned and cut the lining to the same shape as the needlepoint itself. You'll have already added the seam allowances for the article itself so that the lining will come out right if you use the same measurements. To cut an interlining, you make it the same shape and size as the needlepoint's stitched area, and then sew it in place right along with the regular lining. To hold it down while you work, you can put a dab of white glue in one corner. As long as you only use a drop, it won't penetrate to the other side of the stitched area. When adding an interlining, remember that it is placed on the wrong side of the needlepoint, even if you are sewing the regular lining in place with the right side of the needlepoint and the right side of the regular lining facing together.

To sew the regular lining in place, put the needlepoint and lining together so that their right sides face in and touch. Stitch by hand or machine, leaving an opening on one edge that is large enough for you to reach in and turn the article right side out once you finish the major portion of the seam. Then sew the rest of the seam together by hand so that it doesn't show. Linings for needlepoint clothing are very useful since they protect the seams in the needlepoint itself, which have a tendency to come unraveled when they are exposed to wear.

Another method for attaching a lining, used for nonclothing articles such as book covers and the like, is to use felt and cut it exactly to size. Then, attach it with the right sides out, using small amounts of white glue or careful hand stitches. To plan a lining like this, you cut it out to the shape and size of the stitched area itself, minus about ¼ inch, so that it

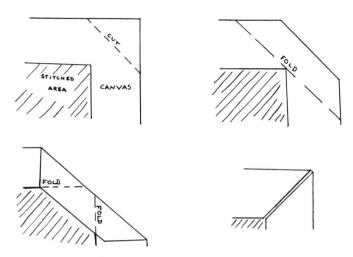

Steps in mitring a corner

doesn't extend beyond the edges of the needlepoint. Then, you put a thin line of white glue around the edge of wrong side of the lining and smooth it in place on the wrong side of the stitched needlepoint, after you have folded the seam allowance to the back so that it is covered by the lining. You can glue the canvas seam allowance down with a thin line of glue before putting the lining in place if it makes it easier to work with. The glue can be used this way in thin lines since it will not soak through the stitches from the wrong side if you don't put on too much. Once it dries, it is strong and flexible so that you'll find it very helpful in assembling articles that aren't going to be worn.

As you fold the canvas to the wrong side in many square or rectangular articles, you may find that the corners are particularly hard to fold. To make them easy to work with, you can make what's known as a mitred corner. A mitred corner folds and lies very flat, so it is a useful thing to know about. To make a mitred corner, draw a diagonal line on the raw canvas corner, so that your diagonal is about ½ inch away from the corner stitches. Cut the canvas on the diagonal line where you marked it. Then fold the cut edge so that it lies flat on the back of the canvas on the wrong side of the stitches and the very corner stitch is visible on the center of the fold. Then, fold the side margins down as usual. You'll find that with the corner prepared as described, the sides fold down to the back neatly and smoothly. You can glue the mitred corner in place, or stitch it along the edge created by the two sides meeting as they reach the corner.

Framing a Needlepoint Picture

If you want to mount your needlepoint in a frame, like a stitched picture, you'll find that it is an effective way to display your work if you leave out the glass. Unless your work is a fairly standard size and you can find a frame to suit it, you should plan to use a frame that you have on hand or have bought before you start to stitch. That way you can plan your stitching to fit the frame by measuring the opening. Then, work the needlepoint the same size, plus ½ inch all the way around to allow for natural shrinkage. To mount the finished work after you block it, measure the inner edge of the frame opening from the back and cut out a piece of heavy cardboard ¼ inch smaller than the actual opening. This will allow for the width of the stitched needlepoint. Place the needlepoint face down and center the cardboard on top of it. Squeeze some white glue onto each corner of the canvas and fold it down to the cardboard backing as you would for mitring. Then, put a line of glue all the way around the canvas edges and fold them down to the cardboard. Check the needlepoint and cardboard to make sure that the work is smoothly in place and is centered correctly and then let the glue dry completely. Place the needlepoint that is now attached to the cardboard into the frame opening from the back. If there are little metal tabs around the edge in the back, fold them down to hold the needlepoint in place. If not, push in some thumbtacks so that they don't show from the front, using the flat kind that will hold the needlepoint in place without interfering with the hanging of the picture.

Finishing and Assembling Embroidery

Finishing and assembling blocked or steamed embroidery is a pleasure. Since it's stitched on fabric, the techniques used to make it up into an article are the same as those you would use for any sewn seam. There are really no special considerations in the actual sewing, other than to be sure that the embroidered motifs are centered correctly before you begin the seams. And, if you are following a paper design pattern, this should be no problem.

After blocking, the margin allowances on embroidery can be trimmed to ⅝ inch, the standard seam allowance in sewing. The lining for an embroidered article that needs one can be cut to these measurements, after you've trimmed the allowance, and easily stitched to the piece. Place the lining and embroidery face to face, pin with straight pins for easy handling, and stitch the seams, leaving an opening as needed to turn right side out. To sew by hand, use the backstitch—see the chapter on embroidery stitches to learn it if necessary. To sew on a machine, set it at about 10 stitches per inch and use a strong thread such as the cotton covered polyester core type, which is also suited to hand sewing. If you have any hems to sew, they should always be done by hand, with a simple overcast stitch that just barely shows on the right side of the hem.

To stitch seams on articles that will receive a lot of wear, do a regular seam and then add another right next to it for extra strength. You can use one of your embroidery needles to sew the seams, and use the thread doubled, as it will be stronger that way. When you've finished sewing the seams, remove the pins and press the seams open with a warm iron so that they are flat and smooth. If necessary, iron lightly around the embroidery, using a pressing cloth if the fabric has wrinkled while you were sewing.

For the pillow backing, you can choose any fabric with the same general weight as the backing of the embroidery itself. If you have enough matching fabric of the backing itself, it can be very attractive to use it to make up the pillow. If you're making a pillow, sew four corners and three sides, and turn it right side out through the opening that you left in the fourth side. Stuff the pillow with a pillow form or loose stuffing material and stitch the opening closed by hand with as invisible a stitch as possible.

To mount an embroidered picture, follow the same procedure as for a needlepoint picture, with the exception that you should make the cardboard only ⅛ inch narrower on each side unless the backing fabric used for the embroidery is unusually thick.

You'll find that the liquid white glue is helpful in mounting embroidery as well as needlepoint because it dries clear and flexible. You can use it for mounting pictures, and adding interlinings for embroidery, as long as you keep it outside of the boundaries of the stitched area itself.

The mounting of embroidery is so much like sewing that most people find it to be a fairly simple task. However, like the complicated articles in needlepoint, such as pocketbooks with a hard frame or furniture upholstery, they should be professionally finished. These are expensive things to do and you will be better off if you discuss it with a good needlecraft shop or other mounting expert before you begin the project.

Care and Storage

Needlepoint and embroidery really don't need much in the way of special care as long as they don't receive unusually hard wear. Their unique beauty increases with time as the yarns, wools, and backings mellow and ripen together.

If they become soiled, you'll find that once they are mounted it's best not to wet them. Use a liquid dry cleaning agent for spot jobs or a spot lifter for small stains. You can also have them professionlly dry cleaned at an establishment that has experience in handling this sort of work. You'll need to do it so rarely that it's best to have it done right.

If you store a finished stitchery, roll it up so that the stitches face out, and keep it in a dark place to prevent fading.

With reasonable care, your needlepoint or embroidery will last for years in perfect condition.

6

NEEDLEPOINT STITCHES

Starting Out Right

Needlepoint, or canvas embroidery as it's often known, can be started with such basic materials that it is a pleasure. As mentioned before, you'll probably enjoy learning the stitches the most if you get a piece of 10-mesh mono canvas, a number 16 needle, and a skein of tapestry or Persian yarn. Use one strand of the tapestry yarn and a full 3-ply strand of the Persian with this canvas. If the yarn comes in a hank, cut it in two pieces and use each strand in that length. If you're using yarn that comes out of a pull skein, find the center strand, pull it out and cut off a piece about 24 inches long. The yarn shouldn't be any longer because you'll find that it will wear out from being pulled through the canvas. If it's much shorter, you'll have to rethread it too often. Cut a piece of canvas about 12 inches square and tape the raw edges with masking tape. Using a completely waterproof marker, outline a 10-inch square on the canvas. You'll work the stitches within this square as you learn them. Until you know the stitches, you'll be better off working without a frame, which can make some moves difficult.

Starting and Ending the Yarn

In needlepoint, the yarn is never knotted at the end, because the knots would cause bumpy places in the finished work. To start and end off the yarn each time you need a new piece or need to change colors, you work the yarn into the backs of a few of the stitches that are already on the

English, 20th century. Maker: Her Majesty Queen Mary. Chair seat, wool on canvas. *Courtesy, The Metropolitan Museum of Art, Gift of Mary S. Harkness, 1948, In memory of her husband, Edward S. Harkness*

canvas. There are two ways to start the yarn on a canvas that has no stitches on it. The first is to leave about an inch and a half of yarn on the back of the canvas and work the first few stitches around it. This method works well when you already know the stitches. While you're learning them it might make it a bit more difficult. To start the yarn in the second way, just run it in and out of the canvas outside of the stitched area, and bring the needle up to the first mesh in the upper right-hand corner.

While you are stitching, to end off a piece of yarn that has become too short to work with easily, complete the stitch you are doing and leave the

Russian stitchery, worked in needlepoint and embroidery stitches on linen
by counting the threads.

European needlepoint
stitchery. *Collection,
Sandra Ley*

needle at the back of the canvas. Slide the needle under the backs of about an inch of stitches and cut it off close to the canvas. If you leave a tail of yarn hanging out, it will get tangled in whatever stitches you try to do in the area, making them very hard to do. To start a new piece of yarn, work it under several stitches right near where you need the new yarn and bring the needle out to the front of the canvas just beyond the mesh of the next stitch. Do that next stitch carefully, as the end of the yarn will pull out of the stitches you just worked it under quite easily until the first stitch with the new yarn has been completed. Again, don't leave a hanging tail of yarn to get caught in the following stitches as you make them. Whenever you can, try to start and stop the yarn in different areas of the canvas. If they are all done in the same place, they'll cause a bumpy surface on the face of the finished needlepoint.

If the Yarn Gets Twisted

As you stitch, the yarn sometimes gets twisted or wound up around itself or the needle. If this happens, let go of the needle and turn the canvas so that the needle and yarn hang down. As they hang there, the yarn automatically untwists and you can then pick up the needle and start to stitch again.

Doubling the Yarn

If you find that you need to use two strands of yarn, for a large-mesh canvas, it's best to cut a strand longer than usual and thread it through the needle. Then, bring the needle to the middle of the yarn and fold it in half with the needle in the center. Then, stitch as usual. This is also true for smaller-mesh canvases, when you would be using two of the plies of Persian yarn. You can use one longer ply and fold it in half in the needle after it's threaded. This method seems to work well since a double weight of yarn threaded in a needle will be quite bulky for the few inches beyond the needle where it will actually be four thicknesses at once.

For normal stitching, you thread the needle so that the yarn is used singly, with only about three or four inches double just beyond the needle.

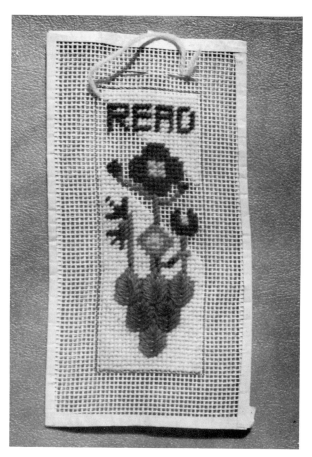

Filling in around a stitched design, using the basketweave stitch.

Filling in a Design

When you are stitching a design, once you know the stitches, you stitch the smallest design areas first. Then, you do the next largest areas and so on, until you complete all of the design units. The background, if there is one that is a large expanse of a single color, is done last. If you try to do it in reverse, and stitch the background first, you may find that the central mesh of the design area have been compressed by the background stitches. This will make them hard to do and easy to skip by mistake. If you do small segments while the canvas is relatively empty, they'll be easier to do. Then, filling in around them will also be simpler.

Following Finished Stitches

A stitching tip is to try to establish a row or two of stitches while carefully following the diagrams, particularly in the textured or patterned stitches. Then, you can use these stitches as a guide to continue stitching without having to refer back to the diagrams, since you'll have a correct version right in front of you to work from.

Counting the Mesh

The counting of mesh in needlepoint canvas may lead to a bit of confusion at first. However, it's easy to do as long as you remember that the number of mesh always refers to the actual threads that make up the canvas. Because the spaces naturally fall in between the mesh, or canvas threads, when you count spaces there will not be the same number. For example, if you have three mesh, there are four spaces, so that you should count the number three as correct. To move diagonally, the term mesh

Needlepoint alphabet, worked by counting mesh, showing how the basic stitch appears in curves and diagonal lines.

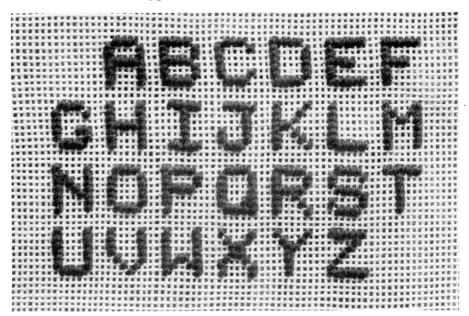

refers to the crossing of canvas threads, so that if an instruction says move one mesh diagonally, it means to count one thread intersection.

Stitch Diagrams

To help you learn the stitches, they are shown here in photographs as completed stitches and in stitch diagrams which actually show you how to do the stitches. To follow a stitch diagram is quite simple, as it is an accurate representation of exactly what should happen on your canvas. The crossed lines in the diagram stand for a precisely equal number of mesh in your canvas, and the stitches drawn on them are shown just as they should look when you make them. To find out how the stitches are made, you do exactly what is shown in the diagram for the particular stitch. To further show how the stitches work, the beginning and end of each stitch is numbered. The number is placed in the space that the needle either came out of or went into to make the stitch, and the numbers go in order, starting with the first stitch. On number 1, the first time the needle comes up to the front of the canvas, you start the first stitch. It is completed at number 2, when the needle goes back into the canvas to the back to complete the first stitch, and so on. Remember that on the odd numbers, starting with number 1, the needle comes out to the front of the canvas and on the even numbers, starting with number 2, the needle goes down into the canvas, coming out the back. If you follow the numbers with this in mind, your stitches will come out perfectly.

Stitch Tension

As you stitch, try to maintain an even tension, or pull, on the stitches. At first you may find a tendency to pull them too tight, buckling the canvas a bit, or to make them too loose, so that they don't look neat. Try to make them like the stitches in the photographs, as evenly as you can. Then natural tension that is most comfortable to you will develop as you stitch, so that you don't have to be too concerned about it as you learn to do the stitches.

Using the Marked Outlines to Count the Mesh

To set up the stitches on the canvas, you usually start at least one mesh away from the actual border of the outlined stitch area on your canvas. To do this, you use the drawn boundary line and count from there. For your sampler and first stitches, divide the 10-inch square you've already marked on the canvas into a series of boxes, either square or rectangular, that you will fill with stitches as you learn them. Then, to count a new stitch area, when you've completely filled in a box, count from the edge of the completed stitches, just as you did from the edge when it was just a marked outline. You do this so that the entire canvas is filled with stitches, without any empty mesh at all. The same is true when you go on to fill a design. All of the mesh should be covered. To check this easily, let a light shine through your canvas. If you can see brighter dots of light anywhere when it's all done, it probably means that you have left out a stitch and you should fill it in with the color of that area in the design. If you've left out a stitch in the center of a larger stitch and there is only room for a small stitch, like the basic needlepoint stitch, do it rather than leaving the mesh empty. It will blend in and look fine in the finished work.

Removing Errors

As you learn to do the stitches, don't worry if you make a mistake. However, when you know the stitches and have moved on to doing a design, you should always correct any errors as you spot them. It may seem unnecessary at the time, but you'll get much more pleasure out of a finished canvas when it is all done well. If the mistake covers a small area right next to the stitch you're doing, unthread the needle and use it to pull out the stitches, one at a time, working backwards from the one you just finished. The yarn will get quite frayed from pulling, so that you should work it into the back of the stitches once you've undone the error, cut it off, and start with a new piece of the same color. If you notice any fuzz still clinging to the canvas, pull it off with your fingers before restitching the area.

71

If you've made a larger error, cut the stitches from the front with embroidery scissors. Do each stitch one at a time and be very careful not to cut the mesh beneath the yarn. Pull the cut yarn out from the back, using tweezers. If you do cut through a single mesh by mistake, pull a mesh from the raw edge of another piece of the same kind of canvas, or untape the edge of the one you're stitching and pull it from there, and then retape it. Take out the stitches around the cut mesh for about an inch and cut an inch off the canvas thread you pulled for this purpose. Dab the two ends of the inch-long mesh in white liquid glue and carefully place it right over the mesh that was cut by mistake. Work the following stitches right around it and it won't show when you're finished. Another method of repairing a canvas that was cut by mistake is to put on a small patch. Take out the stitches for at least a square inch. Then cut a square inch out of a piece of identical canvas, making sure that you mark the patch so that you know where its original side was. If you confuse the sides with the top and bottom there's a chance that it won't match up exactly when you place it on the canvas. Then, place the patch on the wrong side of the canvas. Match up the mesh exactly, keeping the sides parallel to the sides of the canvas. Then, stitch right through both layers. When you've finished the entire canvas, the patched area will not show. If you find it hard to hold the patch in place, you can glue it down with a very small amount of white glue so that it doesn't clog up any of the mesh.

The Basic Needlepoint Stitch

The basic needlepoint stitch is done in several ways, but the different stitches all fall under the general name of tent stitches. These stitches are used a great deal in needlepoint and are what usually comes to mind when you think of what needlepoint looks like. The basic stitches all look alike from the front, or right side, of the canvas. They are the smallest stitch you can make, covering one mesh intersection diagonally, slanting from the upper right to the lower left. How they are formed, and what they look like from the back or wrong side, is what changes in the different stitches. One of these stitches—or a suitable combination of them—is often all that is done to stitch a particular canvas, with the changes in color of yarn creating the pattern or design.

The Continental Stitch

The tent stitch that is also known as the continental, tent, needlepoint, or petit point stitch is used a lot to fill an entire canvas which does not have one large expanse of background in a single color. It can be worked

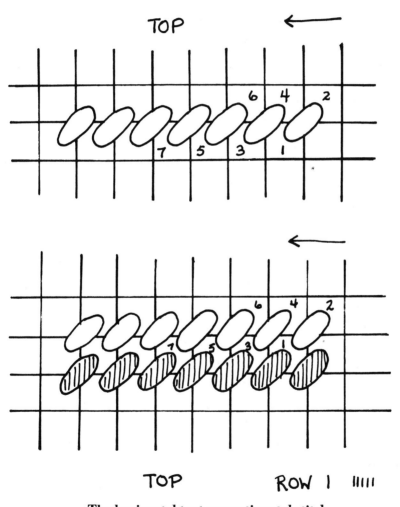

The horizontal tent or continental stitch

73

in horizontal or vertical rows, with the horizontal version being used more often. As you learn each new stitch, fill in the drawn boxes on your canvas one at a time, until you're sure you really know each stitch. When you can do a stitch entirely from memory you're ready to go on to another one, using the next blank box on the canvas. If you use more than one color, you'll end up with an attractive needlepoint patchwork sampler. Even in a single shade, these can be effective when there are various stitches included.

As you do the stitches, remember that the numbers on the stitch diagrams refer to the spaces the needle goes into and out of—which shouldn't be confused with the number of mesh, which are always counted in threads, not spaces.

To begin the stitches, hold the canvas in your left hand, with the threaded needle in your right. If the canvas is too large to hold comfortably, roll it up from the left-hand edge by rolling the left edge under and in toward the wrong side of the canvas. The rolled canvas should be flat on top and rolled underneath, and you can hold the roll in your left hand. The roll should come within two inches of the marked right side border, but not so close that it gets caught up in your stitches.

Bring the needle up to the second mesh from the edge, one down from the top edge, after you weave the first inch or so into the outer canvas to secure the end to reach the mesh just inside the border. Pull the thread through to the right side without pulling its end free. This is actually the first half of a continental stitch. To continue, put the needle into the canvas one mesh to the right and one above where it just came out, or space 2. As you put the needle into the canvas, slide it so that the point goes along the wrong side and comes out one mesh to the left of the first half of the stitch, space 3 on the diagram. Bring the needle out of space 3 and pull the yarn through so that the first stitch forms neatly on the canvas. Don't pull the yarn so tight that the canvas pulls together. Along with your first complete stitch, you have also done the first half of the second stitch. To continue stitching, you always put the needle into the space above and to the right, one diagonal mesh away from where it came out, and bring it out of the space immediately to the left of the one it came out of, one mesh away. That way, you begin the next stitch each time you complete the one you are doing. That's why this stitch is so easy to do. As it forms on the canvas, the back or wrong side is covered with a thick series of larger, more slanting stitches than those on the front. They make this stitch very durable and useful for things that will get a lot of wear.

When you finish a row, complete the last stitch by going into the space one diagonal mesh to the right, moving toward the upper corner. Then, leave the needle at the back of the work, and turn the canvas around so that the top is now the bottom. If you make a mark or write "top" on the canvas' top edge, it will be easier to work, since you must be sure that you've turned it all the way around at the end of each row because this stitch is always done from right to left. When you do the stitch in square or rectangular shapes, it will be easy to see whether you've turned it all the way, as the stitches should always run in horizontal lines. Later on, when you're doing a design, it's not as easy to see and you might make only part of the turn if you haven't marked the top to identify it.

After you turn the canvas, the stitches you just did will run from left to right, with the yarn at the back of the canvas behind the stitch that is now closest to your right. Bring the needle to the front through the space that is already half occupied by the top of the second stitch from the right, or space 1 in the next diagram. Now you can continue the stitches as you did them before, always moving up one mesh diagonally to the right and coming out one mesh directly to the left of the beginning of the stitch. On this row and all following even-numbered rows, the new stitches will share the bottom half space with the stitches of the previous row. In all odd-numbered rows, except number 1, the stitches will share the top half space with the stitches of the previous row. The very last stitch will have its own space if you're making a straight edge. Practice making the stitches so that you don't split or displace the stitches already completed in the row before, for the neatest results.

The vertical continental stitch is the same general stitch as the one you just learned except that, as the name tells us, it is done from top to bottom instead of right to left. You start the stitch by bringing the needle out as if to do a regular continental stitch, space 1. Then, move it up diagonally one mesh to the right, or space 2. The change comes as you slide the needle along the back and bring it out of the space one mesh below the one

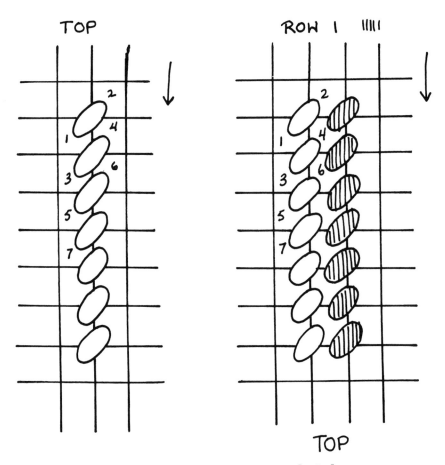

The vertical tent or continental stitch

that began the stitch, space 3. Pull the yarn through to complete the first stitch and begin the next one. To continue, always bring the needle up and over one mesh diagonally to the right, and slide it down and bring it out one mesh immediately below where it came out to start the stitch. At the end of the row, complete the last stitch without starting a new one and leave the yarn at the back. Turn the canvas around so that the stitches you just did run up and down and the yarn comes out the top at the back. Continue by bringing the needle to the front and working as you did in the previous row. On the second and all following even rows, the stitches will share a space to the right, and on all odd rows except the first, they will share a space to the left.

76

Needlepointing on a Frame

If you have your canvas stretched out in a frame or a large hoop, you make the stitches in a different way, although they look the same on the canvas. To stitch in a frame, you use both hands, one on top of the canvas and one underneath. Many feel that stitches done with two hands come out neater, even without a frame. You should try this method after you know the other one well. To work any stitch, keep the canvas horizontal in relation to you, and put the hand you use most on top and the other underneath the canvas. Form the stitches by pushing the needle up with the underneath hand, catching it in the top hand, pushing it down with the top hand and catching it from underneath. You follow all the same steps as in the usual method except that you do them one at a time. On the stitch diagrams, the odd numbers show when the needle moves up, from front to back on the canvas, and on the even numbers, the needle moves down from front to back on the canvas. Be careful on the downward thrusts until you get used to stitching this way, since even the blunt-tipped needle can harm your underneath hand.

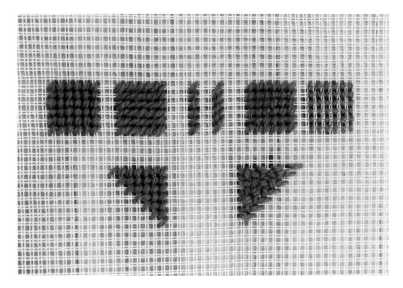

The continental stitch, horizontal and vertical, and the basketweave and half cross stitches, each shown with their back views next to the front views.

77

To work this kind of stitching without a frame, lean the canvas on a table and stitch near the edge, in the space that forms in between you and the table edge. Then use both hands to stitch as just described.

The Diagonal Tent or Basketweave Stitch

The diagonal tent or basketweave stitch is useful for filling in large areas of solid, single colors. It looks just like the continental or tent stitch from the front and like a woven stitch from the back. This stitch distorts the canvas less than the continental stitch does, so that it requires less stretching to be blocked. However, it's hard to work in small areas and is therefore used in combination with the continental stitch in many canvases. The other real benefit of the basketweave stitch is that you always hold the canvas the same way and don't have to turn it around at the end of each row.

To start the stitch, you do a regular continental stitch in the upper right-

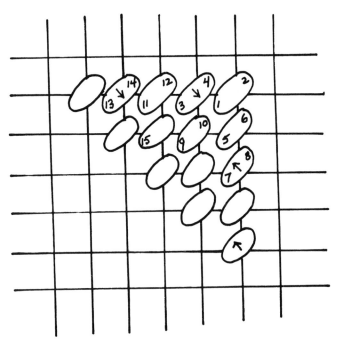

The basketweave stitch

78

hand corner, spaces 1 and 2, bringing the needle out in space 3. Then the diagonal stitch itself begins. Put the needle into space 4, one mesh diagonally above and to the right, bring it out at space 5, which is two mesh directly below number 4, where it just went in. Bring the needle out and put it into space 6, one mesh diagonally above and to the right of the one it just came out of, bringing the needle tip out of space 7, one mesh below the beginning of the stitch. This starts the third row of the diagonal stitch, although it may not seem like it. If you look at the diagram, you can see how this stitch works. On the diagonal rows, you actually leave spaces, one-half a stitch wide, which are filled in on the following row, which then leaves another set of spaces to be filled in and so on. All of the odd-numbered rows, except number one, which was only a single stitch, move diagonally up from the lower right to the upper left. All of the even-numbered rows move diagonally down from the upper left to the lower right. Each time you complete a row, you use the final stitch to start the first stitch of the following row. All of the stitches except this last one on the odd-numbered rows are done with the needle pointing horizontally to the left; all of the stitches except the last one on the even-numbered rows are done with the needle pointing vertically to the bottom as you do the stitch. To see how this works, continue the stitch just begun in space 7. Hold the needle horizontally, tip pointing left, and put it into space 8, one mesh diagonally above and to the right of where it came out, and slide it to space 9, two mesh to the left of space 8 where it just went in. Pull the needle through. Complete that stitch by going into space 10 and coming out of space 11, in the same way. To start the next row, you complete the stitch by putting the needle into space 12 as usual and then bringing it out one mesh directly to the left of space 11. You're now ready to start row four, which is an even row and therefore moves down toward the right. Put the needle into space 14, one mesh diagonally to the upper right of space 13 where it just came out and, holding the needle vertically pointing down, bring it out two mesh below space 14 into space 15. To continue the row always move up one mesh diagonally to the right and bring the needle out of the space two mesh directly below that one. At the end of each row, remember to complete the last stitch while bringing the needle out of the correct space to start the next row.

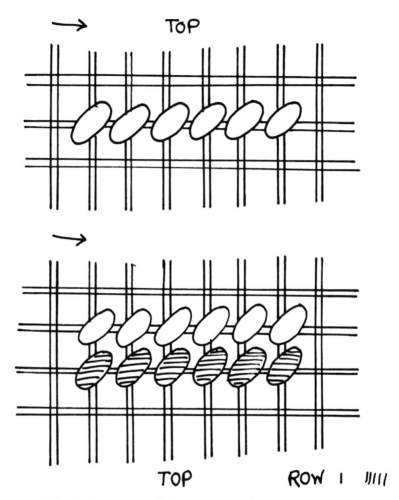

The half cross stitch done on penelope canvas

The Half Cross Stitch

This stitch also looks like the basic tent stitch, but is actually half a cross stitch, which you will see in its entirety later on in the chapter. Ordinarily, this stitch is done on penelope canvas, since it will slip under the single threads of a mono canvas when done over a single mesh. However, if you don't pull it too hard it will stay in place well enough to learn it. This stitch

80

uses very little yarn because the back is made up of tiny one-thread stitches, but it wears out very easily and should be used on the more decorative items that won't get a lot of wear.

To do the half cross stitch, you work from left to right on all rows. This may be welcome news for left-handers. Here again, the canvas is turned at the end of every row, so that it should be marked when you're doing a project. To start the stitch, bring the needle out on the left-hand edge, one mesh down from the top. To do the stitch, hold the needle vertically, pointing down. and put it into the space one mesh diagonally above and to the right of where it came out, and bring it out directly below where it just went in, one mesh down. That's all there is to it. Always go into the space one mesh diagonally above and to the right, and bring it out immediately below it. At the end of a row you do the stitch as usual, turn the canvas, and you're ready to do the next row. In this and all even rows, the bottom half of the stitch will share a space with the previous row's stitches and on all odd rows except the first, the top half of the stitch will share a space with the stitches of the previous row.

Tramé

Sometime you'll see prepared needlepoint canvases with threads of yarn loosely woven into the mesh in horizontal rows. This is called tramé, which is pronounced *tra-may*, and the threads are left in place for stitching. These canvases are quite popular in Europe and are sometimes imported. The loose stitches show which colors to use, much like a painted or printed canvas does in the United States.

This type of threading is also done in any type of work, to pad the stitches. To do it, you thread a needle with the right color yarn and stitch in large running stitches, always moving from one side to the other, not up and down. Cover the area of that color, catching a mesh once in a while to hold the yarn in place, and complete a loose running stitch. When you stitch the piece, you work over and around the tramé threads so that they don't show at all, except in their added bulk.

81

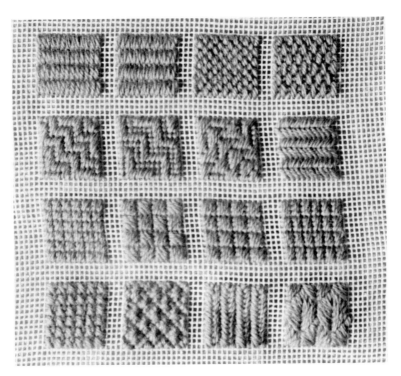

Needlepoint sampler with sixteen stitches

Stitches You'll Want to Try

There is a tremendous variety of needlepoint stitches that add accent and texture to your canvas. They can be used in all sorts of ways for your original stitched designs. You'll enjoy trying them out, as they are easily mastered and, being larger or covering more mesh at a time than the basic stitches, they often go faster while working an area. Most of these stitches are a combination or variation of a few basic stitches, including the continental, half cross, which you know, and the Gobelin stitches, which are presented next. Once you can do these easily, you'll be able to do many of the textured stitches with no problems.

Because you already know how to follow a stitch diagram, these stitches are presented with a minimum of fuss.

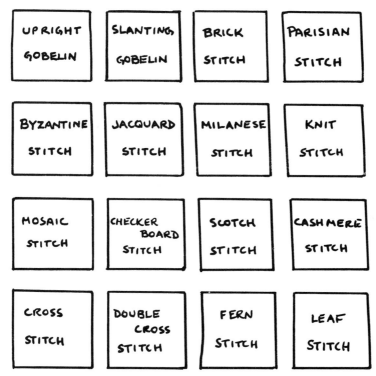

UPRIGHT GOBELIN	SLANTING GOBELIN	BRICK STITCH	PARISIAN STITCH
BYZANTINE STITCH	JACQUARD STITCH	MILANESE STITCH	KNIT STITCH
MOSAIC STITCH	CHECKER BOARD STITCH	SCOTCH STITCH	CASHMERE STITCH
CROSS STITCH	DOUBLE CROSS STITCH	FERN STITCH	LEAF STITCH

Chart depicting which stitches are worked in the sampler.

Straight or Upright Gobelin Stitch

The Gobelin stitches are a group in themselves, used for all sorts of designs, and they are an essential ingredient in Bargello, described in the next chapter. The basic Gobelin stitch is the straight or upright, worked over anywhere from one to six mesh at a time. The version shown here is worked over two mesh. The stitch can also be worked in straight rows, as shown, or in wavy rows, as in Bargello work. It's also a fast way to do borders and backgrounds. It's particularly effective if you tint the canvas, since the meeting spot of two straight rows will have a tendency to show a bit of canvas. It also should be used in only moderate sizes on articles that will receive a lot of wear, because the taller versions will snag.

To do the stitch, you work the first row from left to right. Bring the

83

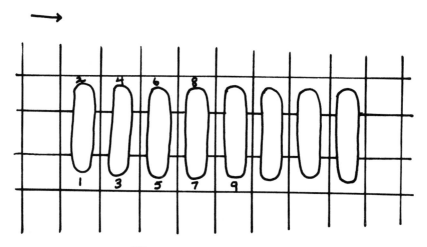

The upright Gobelin stitch

needle out as many mesh down from the top edge in the left-hand corner as you want the stiches to be in height. Then put it into the space directly above where it came out, as many mesh up as you planned for, bringing it out again in the space one mesh immediately to the right of the bottom of the stitch. Do all stitches the same way, for a uniform height within each row. At the end of a row, put the needle into the upper mesh to complete the stitch and guide it down directly below the same stitch and bring it out as many mesh as the height of the stitch below the stitch. Continue the second row by stitching from right to left, putting the needle into the top half of the stitch and bringing it out one mesh to the left of the bottom of the stitch. To reach the next row, guide the needle down below the last stitch as before. On odd rows, stitch from left to right, and on the even rows, from right to left.

Slanting or Oblique Gobelin Stitch

The slanting or oblique Gobelin stitch is done over two or more mesh in height and at least one mesh to the right or left for a slanting stitch. The choice of slant is up to you, as long as it is the same throughout a series of stitches. The stitch is done somewhat like the regular Gobelin, except that you slant the needle to form a slanted stitch. The stitch shown is two mesh up and one to the right, for a slight slant. To do any slanted Gobelin stitch,

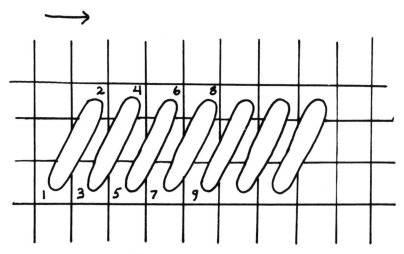

The slanting Gobelin stitch

work the odd rows from left to right and the even rows from right to left, as in the straight Gobelin. Establish the height and slant of the first stitch and do all of the following stitches to match. This stitch can also be done from right to left, like a tall continental stitch, by turning the canvas at the end of each row.

Brick Stitch

The brick stitch is popular for backgrounds and fillings, because it covers well and goes quickly. It is actually an upright Gobelin stitch done on two alternating levels, up and down on every other stitch. It can be done in any height, from one to four mesh. It is shown here over two mesh.

The first and last rows in this stitch are done in what is known as compensating stitches, which help create the pattern without being the same as all of the rows in the middle. This is an important concept to work with, since many of the textured stitches need to have special rows or edge stitches to fill in and help set up the pattern so that the stitch works correctly in the rest of the stitched area.

To do this stitch, the odd rows are worked from left to right and the

85

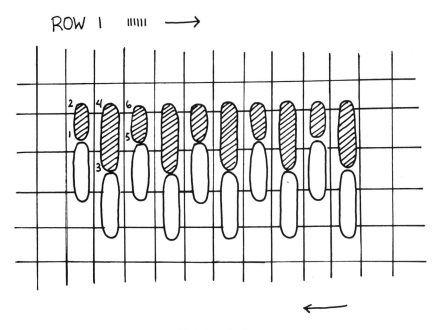

ROW 1

Brick stitch

even rows from right to left. The first row is done to set up the stitch, and consists of one short and one long stitch all the way across. In the one shown, you do a straight Gobelin stitch one mesh, then two mesh, then one mesh, and so on across the first row. Then on the next row, bring the needle out two mesh directly below the last stitch and do a two-mesh straight Gobelin stitch, moving up two mesh and down two mesh all the way across the row so that you fill in the space between the long and short stitches of the first row. On all following rows, there will also be alternating spaces that you fill with more alternating stitches. To do the last row, do stitches of whatever height necessary to fill in the spaces while creating a straight edge along the very bottom.

Parisian Stitch

The Parisian stitch is a variation of the brick stitch that uses one short and one tall stitch throughout. The first and last rows are done in compensating stitches. The odd rows are worked from left to right and the

86

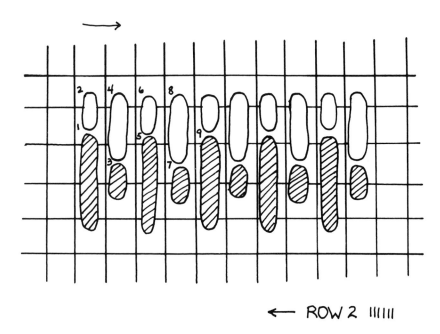

Parisian stitch

even rows from right to left. The first row is done just the same way as you did the brick stitch, one short and one tall across the row. The second and all following rows are stitched so that you work one tall stitch below each short stitch and one short stitch below each tall stitch of the previous row. On the last row you do whatever stitches are needed to fill in the stitch. It can be just one short stitch on every other stitch as shown, or one short and one medium tall, depending on how the last row was done.

Byzantine Stitch

The Byzantine stitch is a zigzag pattern, created by steps of slanting Gobelin stitches. In the one shown, the basic stitch covers two intersections of mesh, and moves three stitches up and then three stitches over, although there are variations that have more stitches in each step.

To do the stitch, you establish one row, moving up from the lower right-hand corner to the upper left. Here again, you need to do compensating stitches, but in this stitch, they can occur on the sides, the top, or the

87

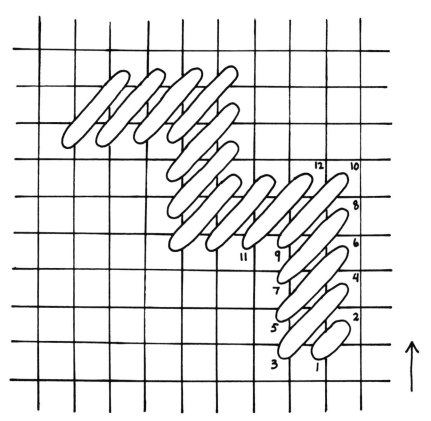

Above and Right: Byzantine stitch, row one and two

bottom. To start, do a single continental stitch in the lower right-hand corner as a stitch to make up for the one that is actually too long to fit within the outline. The first slanting stitch is done above this one, with the needle coming out just to the left of the first stitch and going in directly above its top half. Then you do three more stitches directly above the first slanting one, and continue by doing three more stitches that move to the left, as shown in the diagram. When you reach the top or side edge, you will have to add one continental stitch to fill in for the large stitch which cannot be completed. To continue, weave the end of the yarn in, cut it, and start at the bottom again, moving to the left to continue right next to the beginning of the first row. This row starts with a continental stitch and a set of three slanting Gobelin stitches, as shown in the second diagram for this stitch. Then you do three more above the last one moving up, three

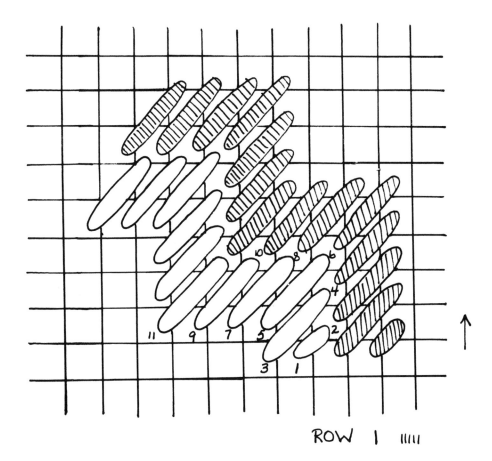

ROW 1 ||||

next to the last one moving to the left again, and so on. When working a large area, complete half of it this way and then turn the canvas around so that you do the second half of the stitches from the bottom up as usual.

Jacquard Stitch

The Jacquard stitch is worked in alternate rows of Byzantine and continental stitches. It is begun the same way except that, in the example shown, the Byzantine part has four stitches moving up and four stitches moving to the left. You then work a row of continental stitches along the pattern set up by the Byzantine stitches. You follow the outline of the completed stitches to work the rest of the rows—one Byzantine and one

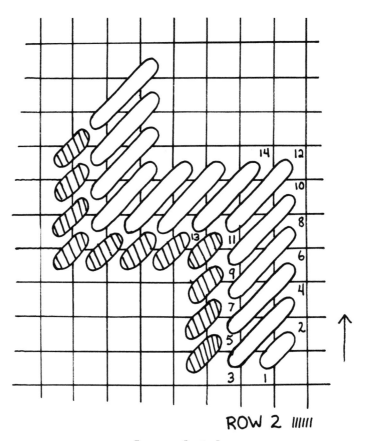

Jacquard stitch

continental—so that it is really the first row that counts because the others will follow correctly if it is correct. To make the fill-in compensating stitches, you'll have to add continental stitches where the slanting Gobelins would usually be. To make them look more like the slanting Gobelins that they're making up for, try making them a bit looser than the rows of continental stitches.

Milanese Stitch

This is an attractive stitch that looks like rows of trees strung together top to bottom. It is worked from the upper left-hand corner diagonally down to the lower right. The stitch is composed of a series of slanting

90

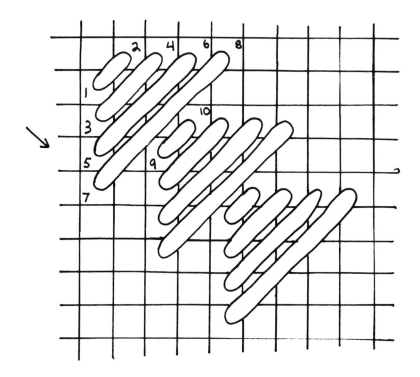

Milanese stitch

stitches, with the first, or top of the tree, covering one mesh intersection; the second covering two; the third, three; and the largest covering four. Then the series starts again with a one-mesh stitch that is placed diagonally below the center of the last large stitch. When you finish an entire row, you turn the canvas around and do another, moving in the opposite direction that fits right into the pattern made by the previous row. The smallest stitch in the second row is placed next to the largest stitch of the previous row, and so on, so that the lines of tree shapes interlock. At the outlined edges and bottom and top of your canvas, you work shorter compensating stitches where they are needed, to fill in the outline correctly when the complete pattern cannot fit in. Along with the Byzantine and Jacquard, this stitch is of the type that comes out very well when done in two or more colors, switching at the end of a row.

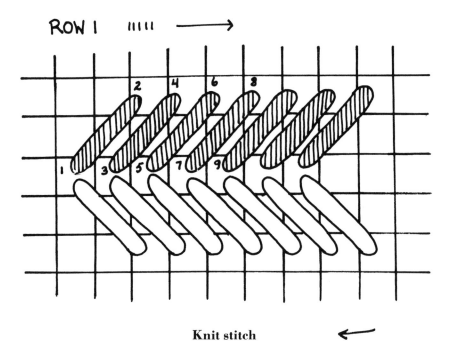

Knit stitch

Knit Stitch

The knit stitch is made up of rows of slanting Gobelin stitches, with every other row slanting in the opposite direction. The slant and height of the stitches is up to you, as long as you do the identical stitch, in two directions for the knit look, on all rows. The one shown slants over two intersections. To do the stitch, you work the first, and all odd rows, from left to right, and the second and all even rows from right to left. It can also be done by turning the canvas at the end of each row, but you can choose the method that seems easiest to you.

Mosaic Stitch

The mosaic stitch is quite popular and easy to do. It creates a lovely texture for backgrounds and filling areas. Each unit of the stitch is made up of three slanting stitches, worked to form a small square, with a continental stitch in the upper left, a slanting gobelin across the middle, and a

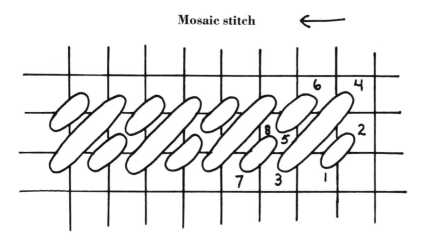

Mosaic stitch ←———

continental in the lower right. There are several ways to work the stitch. The easiest is to work from right to left and turn the canvas top to bottom at the end of each row. Another way to do it is to work from the bottom up, but here again, it's a matter of personal preference.

Checkerboard and Scotch Stitches

The checkerboard and Scotch stitches are versions of the same stitch, using a different slant for the checkerboard. It is probably best to learn the Scotch stitch first. It is very much like a larger type of mosaic stitch. There are also several ways to do these stitches. The one that seems to work easily is to stitch from left to right. Each unit of the stitch consists of five diagonally slanting stitches that make up a square. From the upper left-hand corner to the lower right, the stitches that make up the square are: a one-mesh continental stitch, a two-mesh slanting stitch, a three-mesh slanting stitch, a two-mesh slanting stitch, and another continental. At the end of a row of these square stitches, turn the canvas around, top to bottom, and again work a row, going from left to right.

The checkerboard stitch is a series of Scotch stitches, where the direction of the slant in every other square is reversed. To do the stitch, you work from left to right. Work a regular Scotch stitch, then work the one next to it with the slant pointing in the opposite direction, as shown. Do this across the row and turn the canvas around for the next row, and do a

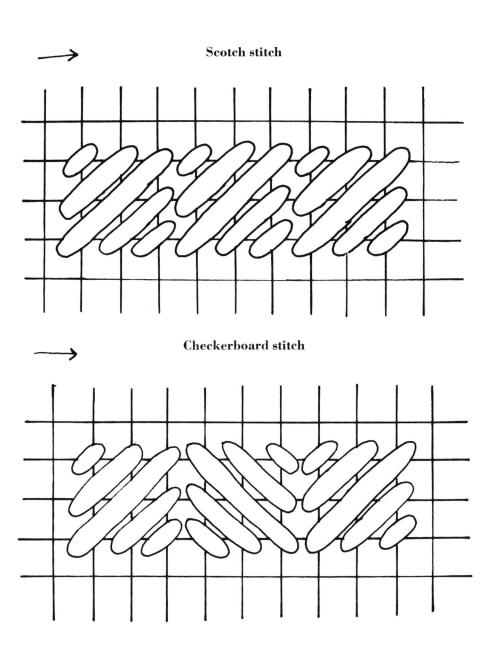

Scotch stitch

Checkerboard stitch

regular stitch over a reversed stitch, and a reversed stitch over each regular stitch. If you make sure that the first square in each row is slanting the opposite way of the one just below it in the previous row and then follow the usual pattern, alternating regular and reversed according to that first square, the entire row will come out right.

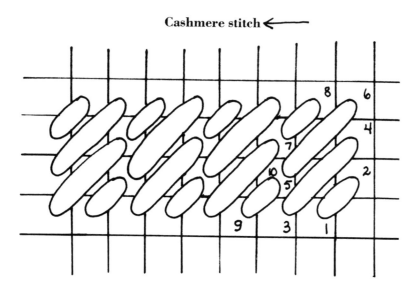

Cashmere stitch ←———

Cashmere Stitch

The cashmere stitch is still another stitch that looks like a variation of the mosaic stitch. In this one, each unit is more of a rectangle, with a continental stitch in the upper left, two slanting stitches below, making up the center, and a continental in the lower right. Since the slanting stitches are the same size, they form a longer pattern that looks more rectangular than square. You can work this stitch from right to left by starting the first unit on the fourth mesh down from the top and working the lower right corner stitch as shown. It can also be worked from the bottom of the canvas up, but this way works well, as long as the canvas is turned at the end of each row.

Cross Stitch

The cross stitch is both fast and easy. A slight drawback is that it doesn't cover the canvas as closely as most other stitches do, so that you may prefer to tint the canvas before starting out, when working a project. The first half of each cross is worked across a row from left to right, much like a two-mesh intersection half cross stitch, which it is. Then, for the second half of the crosses, you stitch a half cross with the opposite slant, working

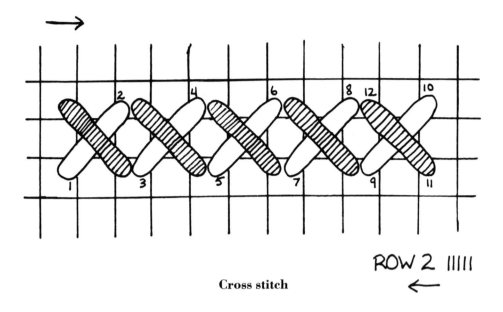

ROW 2 |||||

←

Cross stitch

from right to left. There's no need to turn the canvas, as the stitch moves back and forth as you complete the crosses. As the stitch is made, you hold the needle vertically so that it points toward the bottom of the canvas. An important thing to remember while doing the cross stitch is that all of the crosses should be made the same way for a neat appearance.

Double Cross Stitch

The double cross stitch is done differently than the regular cross stitch, in that each star-shaped double stitch is done at one time and not in parts. The stitch is fairly large, so that you will almost always have to work partial stitches along the edges to fill in an outline. It's best to do all of the complete stitches that you can and then do the compensating stitches when you've finished the rest. One of the essentials of this stitch is that all of the stitches are done in the same order, so that the uppermost cross, which you see when you look at a finished stitch, moves in the same direction each time. This stitch also does not cover a canvas completely and should be done on a tinted canvas or with light colored yarns. The large cross is

96

worked first, and covers four mesh up and down and four mesh from side to side. The smaller stitch is a regular cross stitch, worked all at once, with the stitch covering the center of the larger one. If you could see it clearly, the small stitch covers two diagonal mesh intersections with each cross, as usual. Start in the left corner of the canvas and work the stitch from left to right, completing each starlike cross with the crosses all done in the same way, and end off the yarn at the end of each row. On the next row, you'll notice that there are triangular spaces in between each of the stitches in the preceding row. Start the yarn again at the left and work the second row within these triangles, so that the top half of the stitch fills in the space and the bottom half creates a new series of spaces for the next row. In this way, each row fills in the spaces of the previous row with the top half of its cross. On the alternate rows, like the third, the stitches are done directly below the ones from the first row. It's easiest to cut the yarn and begin again at the left side of each row, because it can be tricky to make sure that all of the crosses are being made the same way if you turn the canvas top to bottom instead.

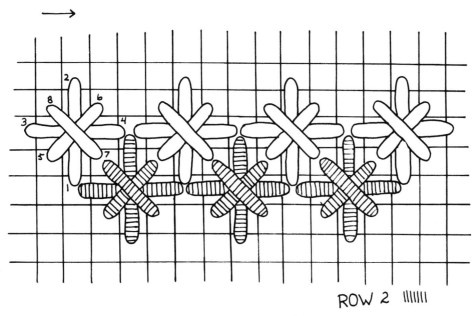

ROW 2 |||||||

Double cross stitch

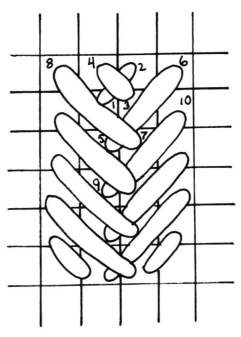

Fern stitch

Fern Stitch

The fern stitch is another type of cross stitch, where the cross occurs in such a way that an interesting woven texture is created. The stitch is worked in rows, from the top down, and you cut off the yarn after weaving it into the backs of the stitches at the bottom of each row and then begin again at the top. Here again, make sure that all of the rows cross in the same direction. The stitch begins with a small cross stitch on the second mesh over from the outlined edge. The stitch itself is crossed in the center and has longer arms than a usual cross stitch. At the very bottom of the row, you do two small slanting stitches, one on each side, to fill in the remaining small blank space in the canvas as shown.

Leaf Stitch

The leaf stitch may seem very difficult at first, but once you get used to it, it's not hard to do at all. It's a very decorative stitch that makes a lovely texture. It's also fairly large and covers a lot of canvas with each leaf. It will rarely cover an outlined area completely but you can fill in the extra spaces with compensating stitches made the way the parts of the leaf stitch would have looked if they had been completed, as shown. Another way to cope with this is to make a bunch of leaves, for a design project, and then surround them with continental stitches to fill in the surrounding areas. The stitch is worked from left to right and ended off at the end of each row, beginning again at the left. It looks good when done in different

Leaf stitch

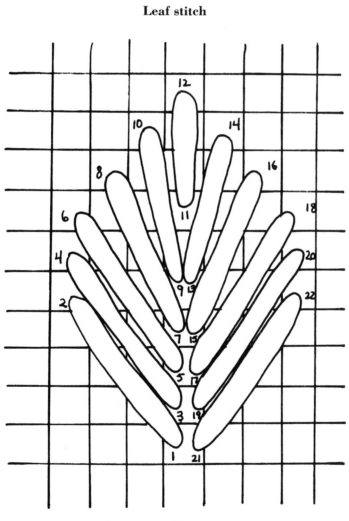

colors and since you have to end it off anyway, it's not too much harder to switch yarns as well. Like the double cross stitches, the leaf stitches fit together on alternate rows, so that the tops of the second row's leaves fit into the spaces in between the leaves of the first row. Once you get two rows established on the canvas, you should have no trouble following them to complete the rows that come afterward. When you begin the first row, to allow for the size of the leaf, start four mesh in and nine mesh down from the top. Then do the slanting stitches as shown in the diagram, with a small center straight stitch for the point of the leaf. After you do a couple of leaves, you'll get used to counting them out and they'll actually become fun to do.

Tips for Left-Handed Stitchers

As you've read the stitches and how to do them, you may have noticed that there is a great degree of variation in how you do the stitches. Some are done from left to right, or top to bottom, or right to left. For this reason, needlepoint does not usually present any special problems for left-handers, with the possible exception of the basketweave stitch, which is done in the upper right-hand corner, without turning the canvas. If you find this stitch impossible to do in the usual way, you can work it by starting it in the lower left-hand corner. To see how the stitch will work this way more easily, you can use that diagram in an upside-down position, where it will look just as if it were done in the lower left instead of the upper right. If there are other stitches that seem hard to you because they are generally worked from right to left, you can try working them from left to right. However, this shouldn't really be necessary, since so many stitches that right-handers do are worked from left to right that everyone who stitches develops a certain flexibility of motion.

Now That You Know the Stitches

The stitches that you've just learned are all you'll need to know to create an endless variety of needlepoint designs and projects. You can use them alone, blended in a group—in short, any way that pleases you—and you'll be sure to enjoy both the stitching itself and the finished product.

7

BARGELLO STITCHERY

Bargello and Florentine embroidery are among the names used to describe a type of canvas embroidery where wavy lines of stitches are done in repeating patterns to create colorful designs. Bargello is probably the most widely used name, derived from what is now a museum in Florence, Italy. It is pronounced *bar-gel-o*, with the g sounding like the g in "get," although many people pronounce it as if the g were a zh, which is not correct. The name "Florentine embroidery" also comes from the same city, so we know that this type of stitchery was quite popular there, even though it may not have actually originated there. Other names you may hear that refer to this type of stitchery are flame stitch or zigzag, but they all mean essentially the same thing.

Basically, Bargello is composed of straight or upright Gobelin stitches, done in rows of repeating wave or flamelike patterns that are then repeated in all following rows. Changes in color from one row to the next create a lovely texture and pattern. The colors are often chosen so that they get lighter and darker, moving through a series of shades in the same family of color. For example, a Bargello might be done in colors starting with white and moving through pink to red to maroon. Many effective combinations are found this way, and even white through several shades of gray to black can look good in Bargello. In other designs, several shades of two colors might be used, with a similar progression bringing each color up to the next. Other patterns can have much more variety in the colors chosen, and this type of decision is up to the individual stitcher. Still other patterns have a series of separate units that are repeated, rather than the rising and falling wavy lines of the most popular stitches. Whichever you choose, Bargello is relaxing and enjoyable to do.

Yarn, Canvas, and Needle

Bargello is usually worked in Persian or crewel yarn so that the strand of yarn can be easily made thicker or thinner to cover the canvas properly. You choose the needle according to how many strands of yarn you need to use for the particular stitch and canvas, which is found through testing on a small sampler. Mono canvas, most often in the 12- or 14-mesh variety is used. You can choose two or more shades of yarn that appeal to you. In general, if you use a 12-mesh canvas, you'll need three strands of Persian or crewel yarn and a size 18 or 20 needle, and for a 14-mesh canvas, you'll need two or three strands of yarn and a size 20 needle. Tapestry yarn will work on the 12-mesh, with a size 18 needle, but you should try it out first to be sure it covers well.

How Bargello Works

To do Bargello, you follow a chart, made especially for this type of work. Otherwise, the canvas is set up and handled as for any other form of needlepoint, with the exception that you do not mark the design on the canvas, only the outlined shape of the entire area to be stitched.

The chart is set up on graph style paper, where the series of small boxes formed by crossing lines on the paper stand for mesh intersections on the canvas. The upright Gobelin stitches are represented on the chart and are done exactly as shown. In many cases, where the entire pattern is set up the same way as the first row, there will be only one line of stitches drawn on the chart. This means that you do all the rows just like the first one, following its pattern once it is stitched. Other stitches, with units of pattern, are done on a single chart by indicating color and row changes with the shade of the drawn stitches. The stitches on a chart like this will be, for example: solid black to stand for one color of yarn, striped to stand for another, and blank or white to stand for a third. You follow a chart like this by doing what is shown for each color at one time and then starting the next color when you're finished with a row or section in the first color. Completely blank intersections on this type of chart are left to show more clearly how the stitches work as you do them, and should not actually be

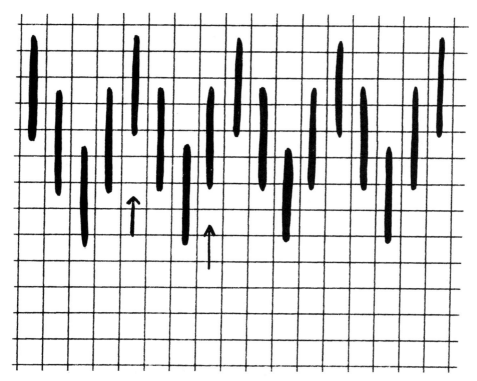

Typical Bargello chart with two arrows indicating one repeat unit.

left blank on the canvas. Rather, when you've finished one whole section, you repeat that section, fitting it into the blank spaces on the canvas.

The Stitch Used

In almost all cases, the upright Gobelin stitch is used for Bargello. It is worked exactly as shown on the chart for the stitch you are doing, covering as many mesh as are indicated by the drawn stitches. The rising and falling pattern of the stitches is also shown. Many Bargello designs use the same number of mesh throughout, so that they rise and fall the same number in each series. For example, in one pattern, the stitch can be four mesh high and move up two mesh each time for four stitches, giving a half pattern, the rising half. Then, the stitch continues, four mesh in size, falling or descending two mesh at a time for four stitches, which will give you a simple zigzag pattern when you repeat the stitch over the whole row and then do all the following rows in the same pattern. Variations are made by increasing the number of stitches done before a step up or a step down, for example, making the highest stitch in the peak three times and then having the same number of falling stitches and making the lowest stitch in the series three times, and so on. Whichever plan is used for a particular stitch, it will be shown on the chart for that pattern. The stitches can also be made in two sizes in one pattern, or slant in another, for more complex designs, but they are always Gobelin stitches, and it will always be clearly shown.

Reading the Chart and Doing the First Row

The first row in Bargello is the most important. Once you've got it correctly stitched, you can usually do the rest without referring to the chart again. For the more complex patterns, two rows or more may be needed to set up the design, but then you can follow them just as easily for the rest of the stitching. For the occasional patterns that are geometric shapes, with central motifs, you can set up the entire network of shapes before working the motifs, or do the motifs and then the network. However, you'll probably find the first method to be the best.

Each chart in Bargello is made to encompass one or perhaps two complete units of the design. Since you repeat this section all the way across, there's no need to show it many times and each unit is called a repeat. This means that the repeat is what you do over and over within each row. Therefore, the chart itself would actually cover only a small segment of the canvas. It's up to you to set up the design for the stitching area you've outlined, by following the chart to work one unit as shown, and then going back to the beginning of the unit and working it from the first stitch again. The units are set up to fit together, so that you repeat the unit as many times as needed to fill the width of your canvas outline. For the smaller design units, you can start at the left-hand edge and work right across the canvas. Count out the spread of mesh between the highest point and the lowest point, and be sure that you start far enough down to allow for one whole up and down motion in the first row. Then end off the yarn and start on the left, underneath the first row, and repeat its outlines exactly in the wave type of designs. When you have finished the entire area to be stitched and can see just how it looks, you work the compensating stitches in the spaces left at the top and bottom of the design. Make sure that you use the colors that would have been there and shorten or cut off the stitches as needed to fill them in correctly.

In a larger pattern, where you want to be absolutely accurate and place one of the major units in the center of the canvas, you begin to stitch the first unit in the center of the outlined stitching area. Count off the canvas to find the exact middle mesh and mark it. Then, count down from the top to be sure you've allowed for the rising and falling of the pattern. Begin the design unit and stitch from the exact center out to the right. Then, turn the canvas around from top to bottom and stitch the other half from the center out to the right again. If you're left-handed you can work from the center out to the left each time if it seems easier to you that way. When you finish the entire row, the next color can start from the border edge. You don't need to start it in the center again, since the pattern has already been set up clearly for you to follow.

For all but the largest and most complex designs, it is usually simplest to start at the edge from the first row onward, for several reasons: you won't have to turn the canvas at all; when you work the row straight through there won't be a ridge in the center of the first row; you'll do all the rows in the same way each time; and, whether you're right or left-handed, you can try starting the design at either border edge to see which method you prefer.

Bargello Patterns

Now that you know how to follow a Bargello chart, you can do any of these designs without any difficulty. Count the stitches very carefully on the first row and check often with the chart and photographs. Do the rest of the pattern to follow, and you can't go wrong. If you want to try several patterns, use a large piece of canvas marked off into large squares or rectangles, or use as many smaller pieces as there are patterns you want to try. You can then make these sample pieces into pillows and other small objects.

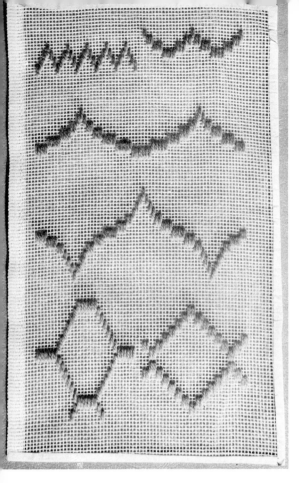

Above Left: Bargello sampler, with the first line worked

Above: Bargello sampler completed. Notice how the compensating stitches are worked at the top and bottom of each pattern.

Left: A Bargello pattern worked in six strand embroidery floss on penelope canvas for a more delicate appearance.

Florentine or Zigzag Stitch

This is the most basic Bargello stitch, for a further bit of name confusion. It is simple but effective, and can be done in as few or as many colors as you like.

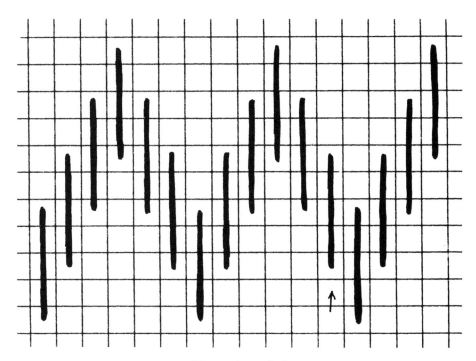

Florentine stitch

Scallop and Wave Stitches

The scallop and wave stitches are quite similar. The scallop covers less stitches per unit, but they are basically the same design, showing how it can change by the addition of several stitches in the center, and surrounding steps. For variety, you can make two or three single stitch peaks between the curved wave stitches.

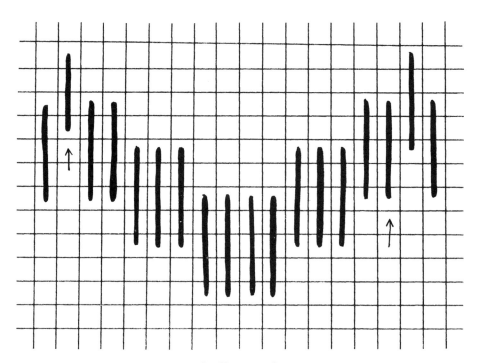

Scallop stitch

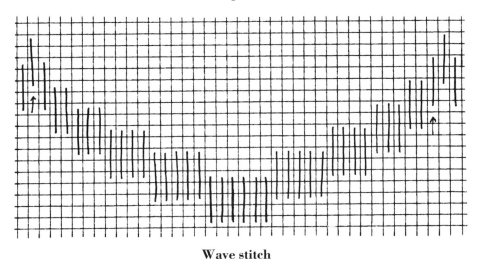

Wave stitch

Peaking Waves

This stitch has a wave pattern that rises and falls, with equally spaced stitches in the rising and falling groups, forming waves with peaks.

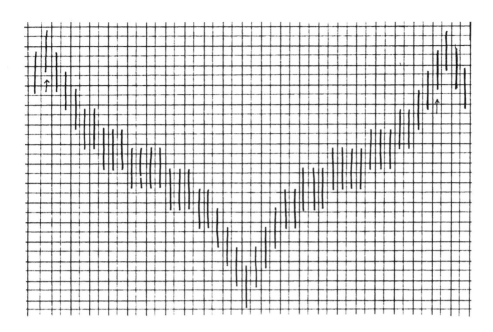

Peaking wave stitch

Hexagons

This geometric shape is done by outlining the basic shapes first. When they've all been done, you fill in the centers. You can change the order of the colors in the center for a different look.

Tulips

These flower shapes are among the few motifs in Bargello that are representative of natural forms. They are, however, stitched in an abstract way. Do the outline first, then the flowers, and their background last.

Other Patterns

One of the exciting things about Bargello is that you can invent your own patterns for it with a little experience as to how the stitches work. Experiment on some blank canvas and see how many patterns you can do, making up your own variations on some of the basic ones that you've just tried. Or make an original. Anything is possible in stitchery.

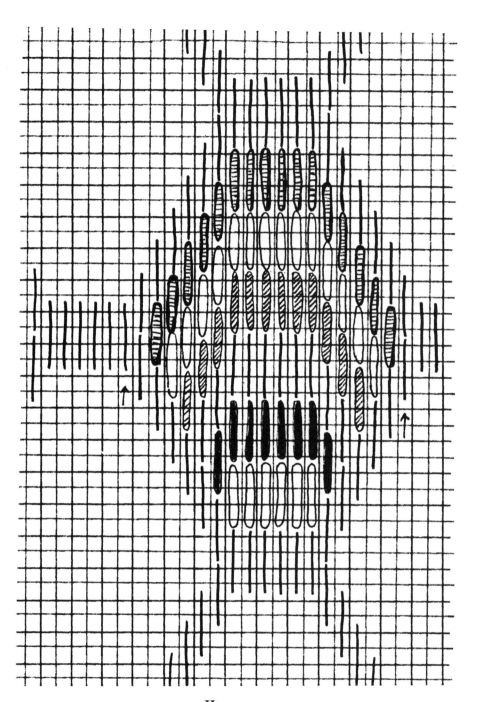

Hexagon

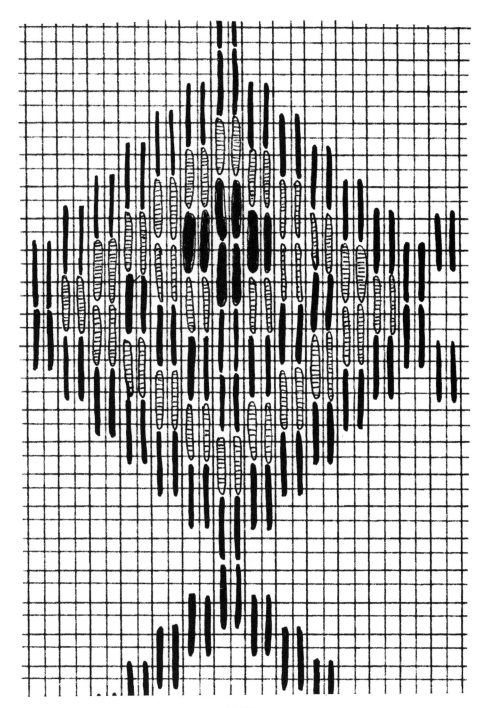

Tulip

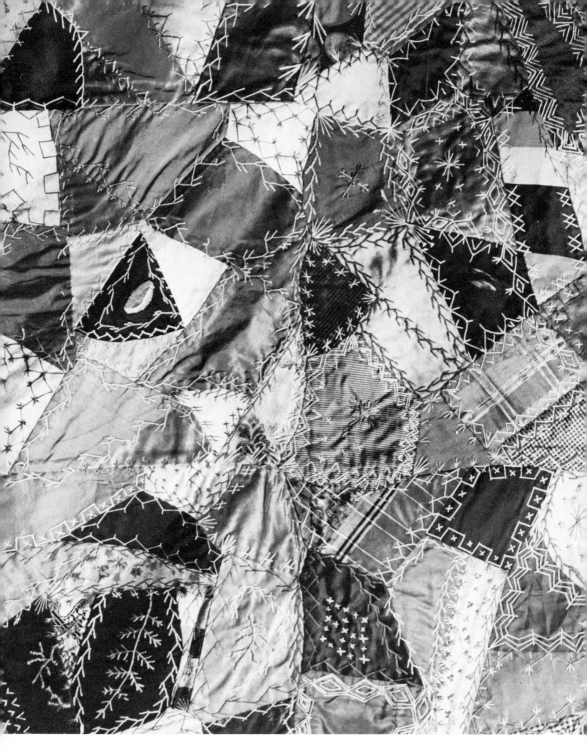

Embroidery stitches on a patchwork quilt. See how many different stitches and variations are used.

8

EMBROIDERY AND CREWEL STITCHES

Embroidery and crewel embroidery stitches look extremely similar for a simple reason: they are the same. The difference between the two is that embroidery is done with either cotton or silk threads, and crewel is always done in wool crewel yarn. The backing fabrics are somewhat variable, to accomodate the weight and fiber of the yarns and threads. Sometimes the distinction is further made that crewel is done in more traditional designs, with less emphasis on free design choices, but this is becoming less true all the time.

Generally, the colors used in embroidery are brighter than those used in crewel, but here again, ideas are changing constantly. True crewel yarns are often found in muted shades that simulate the colors found in old samplers, but you can find lively ones if you look for them. The most usual color for the background is a shade of beige, ranging from off-white to tan or burlap brown, but this too is a matter of choice.

Make an Original Sampler as You Learn

Embroidery, used to refer to either embroidery or crewel embroidery from now on, is interesting to learn, and you can make an original sampler as you learn the stitches. The texture and quality of the stitches themselves are such that they look good on their own. When they are all together on a finished sampler, the results are usually so attractive that the piece is hung or otherwise displayed.

You can make the sampler any way that you want to. Do the stitches

Embroidered floral design: flower petals and leaves in satin stitch, vase in stem or outline stitch, with small flowers in lazy daisy stitch, flower centers in French knots, trellis in couching stitch.

Mexican shirt, embroidered in wool on linen

large or small, in straight lines or curves—it's up to you. One of the pleasures of modern embroidery is this free-wheeling approach, which allows you to express your own personality in all your work, including the sampler. You'll find a lot of pleasure in making it, and when you're finished, you'll know the stitches as well.

To make a sampler, you should choose materials that are easy to work with. For this reason, the traditional linen backing made for crewel and crewel yarn with the right size needle, probably a 3, will be the best to start out with. However, you should not feel limited if you have other materials on hand. They will probably work out just fine. The sampler is what you make of it.

Stretching the Backing in a Hoop or Frame

To do embroidery stitches easily and well, the fabric backing is stretched taut in a hoop or a frame. To place the fabric in a hoop, pull apart the two circles that form the hoop. Place the smaller one on a table and smooth the fabric over it. It should be placed right side up, if there is a right side, and later on, when you're working a design, that area should be positioned as near the center of the hoop as possible. Place the larger hoop over the fabric and smooth the fabric while pressing down on the top hoop to make it fit over the one underneath. If it doesn't go on after you've applied moderate pressure, loosen the outer screw, if there is one. If there is no screw, you may have chosen a fabric that is just too thick for your hoop. Tighten the fabric in the hoop by pulling it from side to side or top to bottom. Don't pull it from corner to corner, which is called pulling on the bias, because it will distort the fabric's threads. Make sure you have the material nice and taut. Tighten the screw a bit if the fabric seems to be too loose in the hoop. As you finish a section of stitching, you can move the hoop if you need to by following the same procedure. Just be a bit more careful with the finished stitches as you replace the hoop if it touches them.

The type of frame you're using influences how you will stretch the fabric to put it in place. Many frames have a cloth tape along one side that you can sew the fabric to, using a strong thread and sewing through the folded border of your backing. This tape is usually on the top, and you use

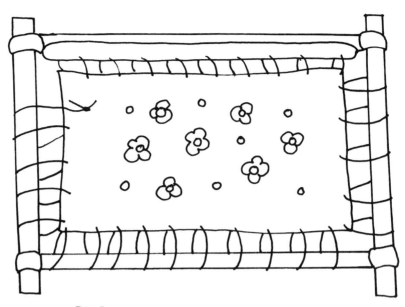

Stitching embroidery backing into a frame

a simple back and forth stitch. Then you attach the sides and bottom with an overcast stitch that you bring all the way around the frame itself before moving on to the next stitch. Since you stitch back and forth between the material and around the wooden bars of the frame, you can use this type of frame even when the fabric seems too small to fit, just by increasing the distance that the thread covers. If the fabric is longer than the frame, you can roll the bottom part around the bottom bar and stitch it in place with a running stitch. Make the stitches fairly large, and stitch through all layers that are wrapped around the frame to hold it in place well. When you've worked the exposed area, undo the top half of the side stitches and inch up the fabric, letting it unroll from the bottom and rolling it around the top. Then stitch the fabric in place to work the newly exposed area, being careful with the finished stitches that are now rolled around the top by leaving the fabric a little looser than usual so that they don't get crushed.

To attach the fabric to a plain frame, such as a picture frame that you've adapted, use the overcast stitch for all sides. Another method for a large piece of fabric, with substantial borders, is to tack them in place on the frame. The fabric must reach the frame with a folded border for this method. You then spread it out evenly and put a tack in the center of each side, being sure that they are smooth and flat. Then continue to put in tacks, working out from the ones that are in place, until the entire fabric is taut and flat. Again, be sure that you don't pull on the corners, which warps the fabric.

Beginning and Ending the Stitches

To secure the stitches, there are two methods. The first is simply to knot the end as you would in any sewing. The other is to take a couple of tiny stitches at the back before starting the stitches themselves, which will usually hold the yarn down. The knotted method seems a little easier and can be used on all but sheer fabrics.

To end off the yarn, bring the needle to the back of the work and take a few small stitches into the back of one of the completed stitches. Before you tighten the thread, catch a loop on the needle. Then tighten and cut it to end it off.

Stitching Techniques

There are two schools of thought as to how to make the stitches in embroidery. You can try each and decide for yourself which is best. The basic two-handed technique is the one favored by most embroiderers, since it creates even, neat stitches and doesn't pull on the fabric. To do this one, you need to have both hands free. If you have a plain hoop, you can lean its upper edge against a table and the lower edge on your lap so that you can use both hands. Of course, if the hoop is too small, there won't be enough room to work in. Place a standing hoop or frame at waist level while sitting.

To stitch, place the hand you use the most on the top of the fabric and the other one underneath. Knot the threaded needle and push it up through the cloth to the front, where you catch it with your top hand. You continue in the same way to make the stitches themselves, using the top hand to push the needle down to the wrong side, catching it with the bottom hand and using that hand to push it up to the right side and catching it with the top hand. At first this may seem very awkward, but once you get used to it, it will work very well. You do have to be very careful when you catch the needle on the wrong side with your bottom hand, since you cannot see where it is going. When you've been stitching for a while you will know where it is going to come out instinctively, but at first, it's all too easy to stick yourself.

In the other stitching technique, you do all of the stitches from the right side of the fabric, with your right or left hand, as the case may be. The stitches are formed by sliding the needle into, along underneath, and out of the fabric to the front again, all in one motion. This will work for most stitches, but it does pull on the fabric and loosen it in the hoop so that you must tighten it from time to time as you stitch. When the backing cloth is very taut, it may be hard to do the stitch right, so you have to find the balance between the two. However, many people do prefer this method and it is probably the only one you can use when you have a small hoop or frame and must hold it in your other hand.

Stitch Diagrams

The diagrams of embroidery stitches almost all look like they are meant to be done with the one-handed technique of stitching. However, this is just the way that they are drawn and is a method of depicting stitches that is fairly widespread. When you are using the two-handed method and use a diagram, to follow it you put the needle down into the fabric where it is indicated in the drawing, and take it with your bottom hand. Then you bring the needle to the spot where it is shown in the drawing as coming out of the fabric and push it up to the front, taking it with your top hand. If you use the one-handed method, you can usually just follow the drawings as shown.

Basic Embroidery Stitches

There are literally hundreds of stitches used in embroidery. They range from simple to ornate, with all manner of variations in between. You'll find that you can do very attractive needlework with only a few basic

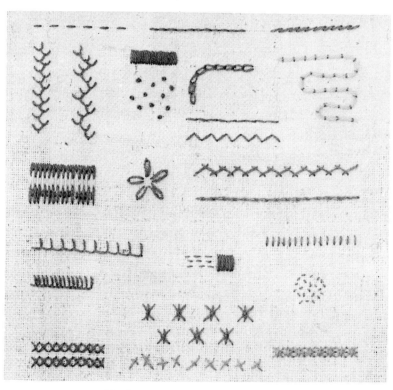

Embroidery stitch sampler

Chart depicting which stitches are shown in the sampler

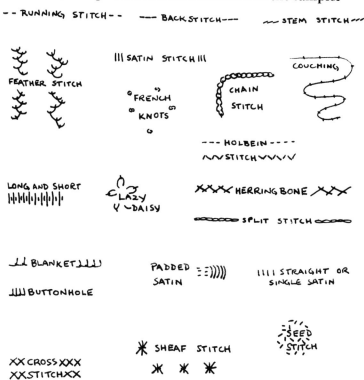

- - RUNNING STITCH - -   - - - BACK STITCH - - -   ⌒⌒ STEM STITCH ⌒⌒

FEATHER STITCH

||| SATIN STITCH |||

° FRENCH ° KNOTS °

CHAIN STITCH

COUCHING

- - - HOLBEIN - - - -
∧∧∨ STITCH ∨∨∨∨

LONG AND SHORT
|ɪ|ɪ|ɪ|ɪ|ɪ|ɪ|ɪ|ɪ|

LAZY DAISY

XXXX HERRING BONE XXX

SPLIT STITCH

⌣⌣ BLANKET ⌄⌄⌄⌄

⌴⌴⌴ BUTTONHOLE

PADDED SATIN ≡≡))))

|||| STRAIGHT OR SINGLE SATIN

SEED STITCH

XX CROSS XXX
XX STITCH XX

✳ SHEAF STITCH
✳ ✳ ✳

X X ✝ RANDOM CROSS   ✳✳ DOUBLE CROSS

stitches. Later on you may want to add others to your stitch know-how that are more complex. As you make a sampler to learn the stitches, do as many as you need to of each one, to be really comfortable doing them. The easiest way to do the stitches at first is along an invisible straight line, unless the stitch calls for a curve in its design.

Running Stitch

The basic stitch in sewing, as well as embroidery, is the running stitch. You may already know how to do it. It's the simple in-and-out stitch, which, in embroidery, is spaced as neatly and evenly as possible, with the spaces in between each stitch being smaller than the stitches but of equal size throughout. For your own stitching, you can make them of any size, in any direction.

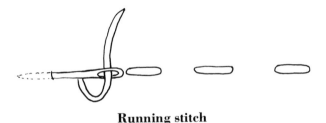

Running stitch

Backstitch

The backstitch makes a filled-in line of stitches and is usually worked from right to left. To do it, bring the needle out a stitch length in front of where you want the first stitch to be. Then bring the needle back to the point where you want the stitch to begin and put it into the fabric, bringing it out again a stitch length in front of the stitch just completed. Continue the stitch by always bringing the needle back, putting it in and bringing it out a stitch length in front, to allow room for the next stitch. This is a strong stitch that makes a good simple line, and it is the best one to use when sewing your work together for the seams, if you do them by hand.

120

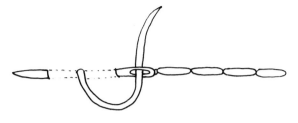

Backstitch

Outline or stem stitch

Outline or Stem Stitch

The outline or stem stitch is done like a backstitch with a slight sideways slant. It's usually done from left to right. To do it, bring the needle out on the left-hand end of an imaginary line. Take it to the right, put it into the fabric on a slight angle the length of the desired stitch, moving the needle back toward the left, and bringing it out so that it is just above the center of the stitch you just made. To continue the stitch, bring the needle to the right a stitch length from where it came out in the center of the last stitch, or half a stitch length away from that stitch's right end. Put it into the fabric, moving back toward the left, and bring it out just above the stitch just completed, in the center of the stitch. You want to get the stitches as close to the center of the previous stitches without actually piercing them. This stitch, as its name indicates, is a good one for outlines and stems on flowers, and can also be used for filling if you make a lot of rows right next to each other.

Feather Stitch

The feather stitch looks more complicated than it really is, and is very attractive. It's done on a vertical line, moving down, and it forms small

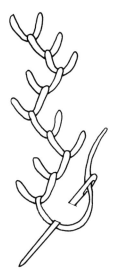

Feather stitch

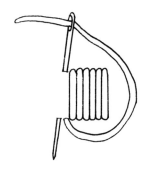

Satin stitch

branches to the left and right as you do it. To begin the stitch, bring the needle to the front and over to the left as far as you want the width of the left branch to be. Instead of pulling the yarn taut, you hold it down with your other hand, forming a small loop that you keep in place with one finger. Then, bring the needle out just below the center of the stitch, and catch the loop of yarn you are holding so that it goes under the needle. Let go and pull the yarn just tight enough to make a smooth curving stitch, held by the yarn coming up out of the fabric. Now you're ready to continue the stitch. Bring the needle to the right, on a level slightly below the first stitch. Put the needle into the fabric and bring it out a bit below where it went in, in the middle of the space in between the end of the last stitch and the beginning of this one, catching the yarn that will fill that space with the needle as you bring it out of the fabric to the front. Tighten the yarn as you did for the first stitch, move to the left, and continue making stitches in the same way, alternating sides as you go. You'll find that this stitch is easy once you do a few for practice, and it looks quite good in branchlike forms and to cover areas with a more open effect. The double feather stitch is done in the same way, with two stitches on each side before moving.

Satin Stitch

The satin stitch is particularly nice when done in smooth yarns with a bit of luster to them, as they will have a sheen when worked in this stitch. It is basically used to form solid shapes out of a block of satin stitches, and can be done in any direction with varying widths. For practice, do it as if you were working in between two imaginary lines and make a "fat" row of stitches. Bring the needle to the front on the bottom invisible line. Take it to the top and put it into the fabric directly above where it came out. Bring it out immediately to the right of the last stitch—or to the left if you're stitching in the other direction—and bring it up next to the top of the last stitch and so on, forming a solid group of stitches. For more complex shapes, outlines are drawn, using any embroidery transfer method. Then you merely stitch across the shape, following the outlines to move from side to side, filling the area with neat, flat stitches. If you want to cover a large area, it's best to make a couple of rows of satin stitches, as really large ones will snag too easily on your finished stitching. Try to make the stitches as evenly as possible for the best results.

French Knots

French knots are small, individual stitches that are actually little knots. They're used a lot in close groups for their crunchy texture. They need some practice to come out perfectly, but once you get the hang of them you'll love to do them—singly, in bunches, anywhere you need some for special effects. To do the stitch, bring the needle to the front, point it away from where it came out, holding it near the fabric. Hold the thread

French knots

123

with your free hand so that it's taut where it comes out of the fabric, and wind it around the needle twice. Still holding the yarn, bring the needle back to where it came out and put it into the fabric right next to that spot. Hold the yarn taut as long as possible while pulling the needle to the other side to complete the stitch. If you have to hold the hoop with your free hand, catch the yarn and hold it taut with the thumb of that hand.

Chain Stitch

The chain stitch is basic to embroidery, as it is the foundation of many stitches that are formed in a similar fashion. It can be worked in any direction, but right to left seems simplest. You can use it to outline or fill in areas, varying its size, once you know how to do it. To begin, bring the needle to the front and catch the yarn so that you form a small loop to the left of where it just came out, and hold the loop in place with your free hand. Put the needle back into the fabric just above where it came out. Bring the needle to the front a stitch length to the left, on the same line as the first stitch, and catch the yarn loop on the needle while letting go of it with your other hand. Don't pull too tightly, which will narrow the stitch, and you'll have completed one chain stitch and started the next. Continue the stitch by putting the needle into the fabric just above where it came

Chain stitch

out, without pulling the yarn too tightly and catching the yarn as you bring the needle to the front again one stitch length away to the left of the last stitch. You don't need to actually hold the yarn loop down after the first stitch, but you can if it makes the stitch easier to do.

More Stitches to Experiment With

You'll find that part of the excitement of embroidery belongs to the wide variety of stitches you can use. Following is a selection of stitches, which you can choose from for new ideas.

Holbein Stitch

The Holbein stitch looks like a neat backstitch when it is done and is very often worked in a zigzag design, possibly in two colors. To do it, you make a series of running stitches, spacing them the same distance apart, as they are long, working from right to left. Then, working from left to right, you do running stitches in the spaces left by the previous line of stitches. For a zigzag, slant all of the first stitches one way and all of the next stitches in the other way as you fill them in.

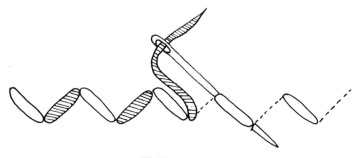

Holbein stitch

Couching Stitch

When you do couching, you sew down a thread or heavy yarn that is placed on top of the fabric with small stitches in a lighter yarn. It can also be used for unusual items, such as thin strips of wood, bark, leather, or straw that could not be sewn on in any other way. It's an inventive technique for this reason. To do it, place the object to be sewn in place on the fabric, and stitch carefully around it with small stitches in another thread. For further interest, you can use yarns of different colors for couching.

Couching stitch

125

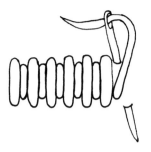

Long and short stitch

Long and Short Stitch

The long and short stitch is actually a form of satin stitch. It's used for filling larger or more unusual shapes than you could with a regular satin stitch. To do it, you stitch alternating satin stitches, one long and one short, as the name states. On the next row of stitching, you work one long stitch under each short one of the previous row and one short stitch under each long stitch of the previous row. This stitch is quite popular for making flowers and leaves with a solid look and may be done in a series of yarn colors so that the shapes are shaded, from light to dark or dark to light, somewhat as they would be in nature.

Lazy Daisy or Detatched Chain Stitch

The daisy stitch is a series of single chain stitches done in a circle so that they look like a flower. The difference between this and the chain stitch is that you sew down each loop with a small stitch in the center instead of continuing the chain. To do it, bring the needle to the front, catch a loop of yarn with your other hand, bring the needle around, and put it in right next to where it came out, bring it back out in the center of the loop. Let go of the loop, close the stitch by bringing the needle just over the yarn and making a small stitch to hold the loop in place. Continue around in a circle to complete the daisy. An effective combination is to put one or more French knots in the center for a real daisy look.

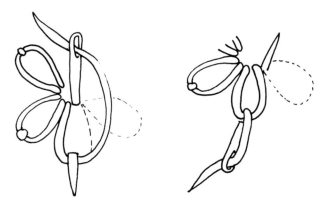

Lazy daisy stitch

Herringbone Stitch

The herringbone stitch is an open crossing stitch, worked from left to right, although the needle moves from right to left as you do it. It is planned along a double imaginary line, one above the other. To do the stitch, bring the needle to the front on the lower left line, where you want the stitches to begin. Put the needle into the fabric on the top line, a stitch length over to the right. Bring the needle out to the front, a bit to the left of where it went in on the top line, running along the same line. Take the needle to the bottom line, as far to the right as the one you just did, put the needle into the fabric and bring it out just a little to the left, running along the same bottom line, the same small distance that you moved the needle back along the top line in the stitch before. You've now completed one stitch, which should look like an X. Continue to make the following

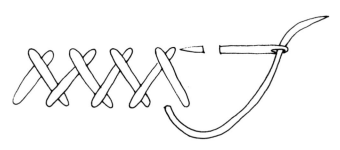

Herringbone stitch

stitches in the same manner, alternating top and bottom so that the stitch looks like a series of X's with their tips crossed. When you know the stitch, you can vary it by making it taller or wider, however you think it looks best.

Split Stitch

The split stitch looks like a fine chain stitch. It covers the fabric nicely and is well done in close rows for filling, or in single rows for outlines. It is worked very much like a backstitch. To do it, work from left to right. Bring the needle to the front of the fabric, at the left end of an invisible line. Bring it to the right, put it into the fabric and bring it out a bit to the left, as if you were doing a small backstitch, but as you bring the needle out of the fabric, put it through the yarn so that it splits the yarn in half. Pull the yarn all the way through and continue the stitch by taking the needle to the right, making a small backstitch and putting the needle through the yarn as you bring it to the front to complete the stitch.

Split stitch

Blanket and Buttonhole Stitches

The blanket and buttonhole stitches are actually the same stitch. The only difference is that the blanket stitch is done farther apart so that you can see the actual stitches more clearly, and the buttonhole stitch is done

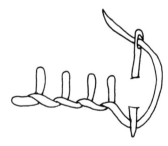

Blanket stitch

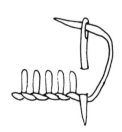

Buttonhole stitch

128

in closer, more solid looking rows. It is done from left to right, following two imaginary lines that run along next to each other, from left to right. Bring the needle to the front on the lower left line, where you want the stitches to begin. Then bring the needle up to the right. Put it into the fabric without tightening the stitch, bring it out on the lower line, directly below where it just went in, and catch the yarn on the needle as you bring it through to the front. Continue the stitch by moving up the right, putting the needle in, and bringing it out directly underneath and catching the yarn on the needle as you bring it out each time. To do the buttonhole stitch, merely move less to the right on the top line on each stitch.

Padded Satin Stitch

The padded satin stitch is done to add bulk and a raised texture to the satin stitch. To do it, you just fill in the area to be covered by satin stitches with small running stitches placed very close together. Then stitch the satin stitch right over and around them as if they weren't there.

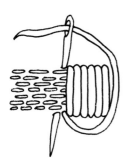

Padded satin stitch

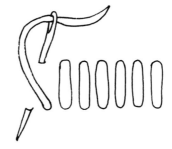

Straight stitch

Straight Stitch or Single Satin Stitch

The straight or single satin stitch is done quite often as a filling or background stitch. It looks like a series of parallel running stitches or open-spaced satin stitches. You do it just like the satin stitch, leaving space in between each stitch instead of making them close together.

129

Seed Stitch

A popular filling stitch, the seed stitch consists of lots of small straight stitches done at different angles to each other. Each stitch is made the same length as the others, but moving in a different direction. You usually outline an area to be filled with seed stitches, with the stem or split stitch, or any other outlining stitch.

Seed stitch

Sheaf Stitch

The sheaf stitch is also used to fill in an area, and it looks like a bundle of wheat. It is usually spaced along imaginary rows in an organized fashion. To do it, imagine two horizontal rows and make three single satin stitches between the lines, without pulling them completely flat against the fabric. They should be almost flat, but not quite. Then bring the needle to the front on the left side of the center of the center stitch and slide the needle under the outer left stitch and then around to the right and under to right-hand stitch. Put it into the fabric right next to the spot where it just

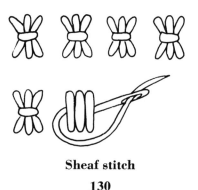

Sheaf stitch

came out, and pull the stitch from the wrong side so that the three stitches are joined by the center stitch. Space the next sheaf and all that follow so that they are neatly lined up in rows.

The Cross Stitch—A Style of Its Own

The cross stitch is often used alone to create an entire stitchery. This was done a great deal on a certain style of sampler in times past, and usually consisted of mottoes and sayings worked in cross stitches, as well as the alphabet samplers. It's best to do it on a fabric with an even weave, so that you can make each stitch the same size as all of the others by counting the threads of the fabric. Another fabric that's used for cross stitch designs is checked gingham, where you can do each cross stitch to cover a single check. As you work the stitch in the corners, you'll be able to see where a perfect cross stitch is without counting.

Cross Stitch

The cross stitch is worked in rows, from right to left for one-half of the stitch and from left to right on the return trip, to complete the stitch. You can reverse this order if it's easier for you to work from left to right on the first half, when you're setting up the stitches. It is worked following two imaginary lines. If you're counting threads, they should be as far apart as you want to make the stitches, and then you count out the same number to find out how wide to make them as well. To do the stitch, bring the needle

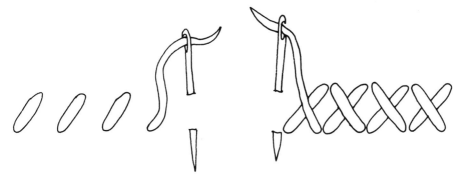

Cross stitch

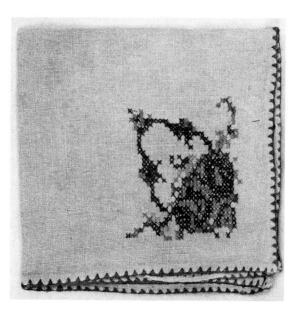

Embroidery worked entirely in cross stitch

out on the lower right line, where you want the stitches to begin. Move it to the left on a diagonal, put it into the fabric on the upper left line, pointing down and bringing it to the front again, directly underneath, on the lower line. That makes half a cross stitch and you continue along the row, putting the needle in on the top line and bringing it out directly below on the bottom line moving to the left. At the end of the row, do the stitch as usual, bringing the needle out as usual, then moving it to the right and putting it into the fabric immediately to the left of the top of the stitch to the right, and bringing it out directly below, a tiny bit to the right of the bottom of the last stitch. This will complete one cross and begin the second half of the next one. Continue across the row in the same way, moving the needle to the right and putting it in on the top line and bringing it out on the bottom. Make sure that all of the stitches are the same size and that they all cross the same way in any one work.

Random Cross Stitch

The random cross stitch is used in more free-style work, with each stitch bring made at one time. To do this stitch, you can make the crosses any

132

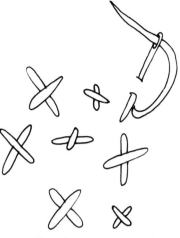

Random cross stitch

size and shape, without even matching the two halves of the stitch. It makes an interesting filling for large areas, and is easy and fun to do.

Double Cross or Star Stitch

The double cross, or star stitch, is a more ornate stitch than is used in regular work and is sometimes used for variety on cross stitch work. It is done with each stitch being completed at once, and as you do it you imagine that you are working within a square. Do a regular cross stitch, from upper right corner to lower left and upper left to lower right corners. Then, cross that stitch by bringing the needle out of the center edge on the right and putting it in on the opposite edge on the left. Finish the stitch by making the last cross, from center top edge to center bottom edge. Do all the stitches so that they cross the same way. For variety, you can make the top upright cross twice as large as the one underneath, or do the stitch in two parts, using two different colors of yarn for the top and bottom crosses.

Double cross stitch

9

LET'S STITCH

Now that you know the basics of needlepoint and embroidery, the following projects will help you to gain a real working knowledge of these arts. And you'll enjoy them all the more as you create practical, attractive articles.

As you do each project, you can refer to the chapters on patterns and procedures, needlepoint, Bargello, or embroidery, if you need to refresh a particular stitch in your mind or to check on the method of enlarging or transferring designs onto canvas and cloth.

The materials that you should have on hand to make any of the articles are tracing and plain paper to set up designs and patterns, pencil, ruler, waterproof marking pens, carbon paper or transfer pens, masking tape, white glue, various sized needles, and strong sewing thread. With these items you'll have no trouble in planning and executing anything that you want to make. They'll also be invaluable to you for creating your own patterns and designs.

In general, to do each project you should first make a paper pattern, to follow while stitching and to use to outline your backing fabric or canvas. Trace and enlarge the patterns and designs as shown for each article. If you're planning an article that must fit such as a scissors case, use the paper pattern to make sure that the finished article will fit your scissors. If it is too large or too small, you can make the needed adjustments on the paper before you begin to stitch the item itself. All of the patterns shown have the seam and shrinkage allowances built in, but if you create your own or need to change one of these, remember to make the necessary allowances in your version.

Now that you know just what to do—let's stitch.

Bookmark

To make a bookmark, you need a small piece of canvas, 5 inches by 9 inches, some felt for a backing, and less than a skein of yarn. Since you don't need much yarn, this is a good project to use up odds and ends of

Bookmark. Background worked in basketweave, outline in vertical and horizontal continental stitch, flower centers in mosaic stitch, leaves in leaf stitch, flowers and stems in continental stitch.

Diagram of bookmark

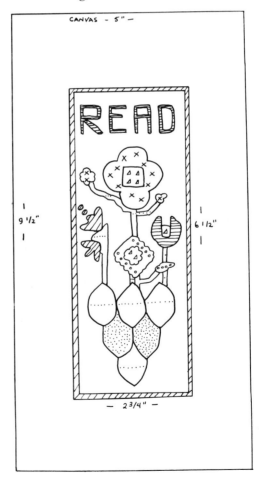

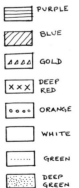

PURPLE

BLUE

GOLD

DEEP RED

ORANGE

WHITE

GREEN

DEEP GREEN

yarn that you have on hand. The canvas shown is 10-mesh. Remember that if you choose a different size mesh, the same design will come out differently, because you will have more or less stitches to the inch than in the bookmark shown.

Place masking tape on the cut edges of the canvas, copy the design on paper, and then copy it onto the canvas. Block when finished. Cut a piece of felt to use as a backing, the same shape as the stitched area minus ⅛ inch all the way around. Trim the excess canvas and fold the remaining margins to the wrong side of the stitched area, securing in place with a very thin line of white glue. Then run another thin line of white glue around the glued canvas margin and smooth the felt lining in place. Let dry completely. Place the bookmark in between two heavy books when it's almost dry, to flatten it a bit and make it less bulky.

Crewel Pin Cushion

This is a crewel project that uses a small amount of yarn and fabric. The fabric used should be sturdy but not so tightly woven that it's hard to put

Porcupine crewel pin cushion

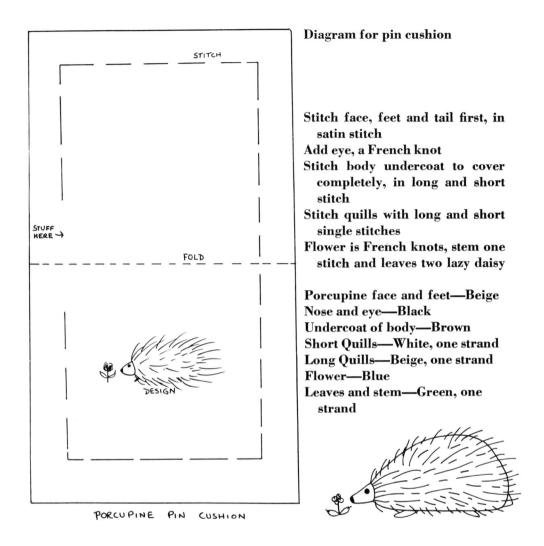

Diagram for pin cushion

STITCH

STUFF HERE →

FOLD

DESIGN

PORCUPINE PIN CUSHION

Stitch face, feet and tail first, in satin stitch
Add eye, a French knot
Stitch body undercoat to cover completely, in long and short stitch
Stitch quills with long and short single stitches
Flower is French knots, stem one stitch and leaves two lazy daisy

Porcupine face and feet—Beige
Nose and eye—Black
Undercoat of body—Brown
Short Quills—White, one strand
Long Quills—Beige, one strand
Flower—Blue
Leaves and stem—Green, one strand

pins into it when it's finished. Outline the area to be stitched and then mark the design on the fabric. To use a hoop most easily, cut out the actual shape for the front and back of the cushion after you've completed the stitching, and the steaming or blocking, if needed. Then, place the right sides of the now cut-out shape together and sew them with a back-stitch. Go almost all of the way around, but leave enough of an opening to turn it right side out. Stuff it as firmly as possible with shredded foam, kapok, or other loose stuffing material, and then stitch the opening closed.

Bargello Change Purse

This handy change purse is made out of a single strip of 12-mesh canvas that is stitched and folded to form the purse. The canvas should be at least 11 inches by 7 inches. This purse is stitched in several shades of imported tapestry yarn that comes in small skeins, so that many colors can be used in a pattern. If you buy larger, 40-yard skeins, three will be more than enough, although you can get another skein for more color if you like, since there is always a use for extra yarn, in small projects, samplers, and patchwork stitcheries. You'll also need a medium-sized snap fastener to sew on, as a means of closing the purse, and a piece of felt for the lining.

Prepare the pattern and stitch. You may not need to block it, since Bargello often doesn't distort the canvas, due to the straight stitches, but if you do need to, block it. Cut a strip of felt the shape and size of the finished stitched area, minus ⅛ inch all around. Sew the top half of the snap to the felt where the mark is shown on the pattern. Trim the edges of the canvas and fold to the wrong side, being sure to have a row of stitching just going over the edge, so that the canvas doesn't show. Sew the bottom half of the snap to the right side of the stitched area, where shown. Place the lining on the stitching, making sure that the snap top is facing out. Put in a couple of straight pins to hold the two pieces together and fold on the fold lines shown in the pattern so that you can see where the sides meet the middle of the strip. Mark the point where they meet at the top, where they come together, with two pins. If the lining seems too long when the purse is folded, or sticks out of the sides at all, trim it. Unfold the purse again. Then, thread a sharp-pointed needle with one of the colors that you used in the pattern. Stitch the bottom edge of the purse with a simple overcast stitch that comes out a bit below the edge of the fabric, then goes up over the top of the edge and into the fabric again. Make sure that you stitch the edge and the lining together. End it off. Then, start to stitch again from the first pin, which marks the spot where the bottom met the sides when folded. Stitch up, away from the pin, around the top, and down the other side to the pin marking the same spot on that side. Fold the bottom half up to the side again and stitch down, sewing all of the canvas

Above: Bargello change purse

Right: **Dimensions and fold lines of change purse canvas**

+SNAP TOP

2"

4"   9"

3"

X SNAP BOTTOM

- 4" -

- CANVAS 7" -

CUT LINING IN STITCHING AREA SHAPE

Below: Bargello pattern for the purse

REPEAT ROW AS NEEDED FOR LENGTH
WIDTH • 4 1/8 inches ON 12 MESH CANVAS

and lining together. End off from inside the now half-sewn purse. Sew the other side from the bottom edge up to the pin and end off. Remove the pins and fold down the top. As your snaps are already in place, your purse is finished.

139

Pen and Pencil Case

To make a stitched pen and pencil case, you'll need a piece of strong fabric, one foot square, and a 7-inch zipper. As in most crewel work, you'll need a small amount of yarn, less than one whole skein for the entire project. Don't actually cut the parts or sew the fabric until after stitching, as usual. Mark the outlines, design, and stitch it. Steam if needed.

To assemble the case, put in the zipper along the shorter two edges of the material, as directed on the zipper package. Then, open the zipper and place the right sides of the fabric together. Pin in place. Stitch the remaining sides' seams together, using the backstitch or a sewing machine. Then, turn it right side out through the zippered opening.

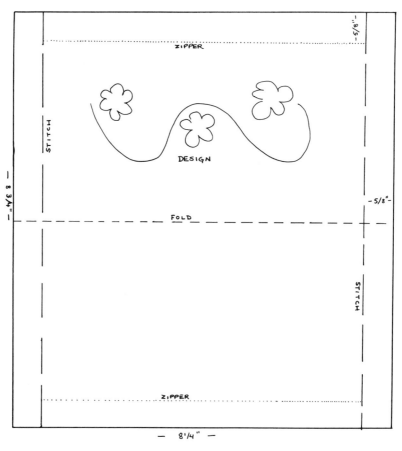

Dimensions and fold lines for the backing for the case

Embroidered pencil case

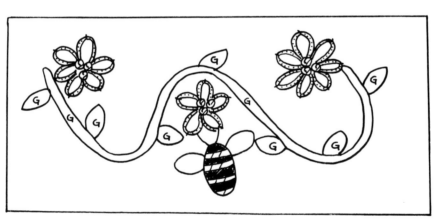

STEM - CHAIN STITCH
PETALS - LAZY DAISY
FLOWER CENTERS - FRENCH KNOTS
LEAVES, BEE WINGS AND BODY -
SATIN STITCH

WHITE
G GREEN
PINK
GOLD
BLACK

Stitchery design for the front panel of the pencil case

141

Needlepoint Forest Scene

These trees make a nicely balanced design that looks quite good when framed as a needlepoint picture. They're stitched on 10-mesh penelope canvas, with tapestry yarn. You'll need one skein of light blue, one of brown, one forest green, one olive green, and one light green. The canvas should be a foot square.

Mark the canvas as usual and stitch it in the design, using the colors as shown. Block the finished work. You may need to block it twice, since the continental stitch used for this work tends to pull it out of shape quite badly, although you can restore it to its original square shape. Mount the canvas for a picture frame as described in Chapter 5. If you have a frame that is larger than the stitched area, there is another way to mount it, which will be effective for this design. Cut out a piece of cardboard to fit the opening of the frame precisely. Place the canvas on it, centering it on the cardboard, and mark its outlines on the cardboard. Then, take it off and mark the stitched area itself. Get a sheet of really heavy paper with a good texture, such as Bristol board, or oak tag for a shinier surface. Measure the area around the stitched area that was marked off on the cardboard. You should place the ruler just inside the stitched area and measure right out to the edge of the cardboard. Then mark off these measurements on the wrong side of the sheet of heavy paper. Cut out the center of the paper without cutting through the remaining area, so that you are left with a sort of square doughnut-shaped sheet of paper that is one continuous piece. Place the canvas back on the cardboard and glue its margins flat to the board. Let dry and place the open centered sheet of paper on top of it. Glue it down to the cardboard at the inside corners. Place the entire piece into the frame and secure as usual. You now have a needlepoint piece, framed to fit a larger frame with an attractive border around the stitched area, setting it off from the frame nicely.

Needlepoint forest scene. Designed and stitched by Sandra Ley.

Diagram of scene, completely worked in basketweave or continental stitch

BRIGHT GREEN △

LIGHT GREEN ✕

OLIVE GREEN ○

BROWN

LIGHT BLUE

Stitch a Pocket

One of the most interesting ways to use embroidery is to add decorative touches to a plain piece of clothing.

This tree was stitched on the pocket of a light blue chambray shirt, using a 3-inch diameter hoop to separate the pocket from the body of the shirt while stitching so that the pocket wasn't stitched shut. You can also stitch a design in lots of other places on a shirt, without having to work in such close quarters. A small design on cuff, collar, or the back would be other places you could stitch a pattern.

For this design, six-strand embroidery floss was used, in brown, red, and

Pocket stitchery

APPLES AND LEAVES IN SATIN STITCH
TREE TRUNK AND BRANCHES IN LONG AND SHORT STITCHES

RED APPLES ●

GREEN LEAVES ⬭

PALE GREEN LEAVES ○

BROWN TRUNK AND BRANCHES

Diagram for pocket stitchery

four shades of green. As it is inexpensive, the leaves are more exciting when done in various greens. The apples are, naturally, red. After you copy the design onto the area to be stitched, you should stitch the trunk of the tree first. All six strands of floss were used for the trunk and branches. The apples and then the leaves were stitched, each using three strands of floss. In a design such as this one, with many very small segments, you can fill in the apples and the leaves pretty much as you please, once the trunk and branches are done. There's no need to follow the design precisely. The leaves, in particular, seem to work out differently as they're stitched. It is important to do them in the order given, since things look more natural when the areas that would actually be covered, such as the branches, are stitched first, then the apples, and the leaves last. Steam from the wrong side when finished.

Covered Container

This useful container is a covered coffee can. The design was developed out of the wave Bargello pattern on 14-mesh canvas. It's a good desk accessory and saves an item that might normally be thrown away for practical use. This pattern just didn't cover well with two strands of Per-

Covered container, in Bargello "Dancing Dirt" design

One unit of the Bargello flower, diagram to be repeated as needed to cover area

GREEN   DARK GREEN   LIGHT BLUE

BROWN   WHITE   PINK

MAROON   YELLOW   GOLD

I FOUR MESH STITCH   ½ STITCH

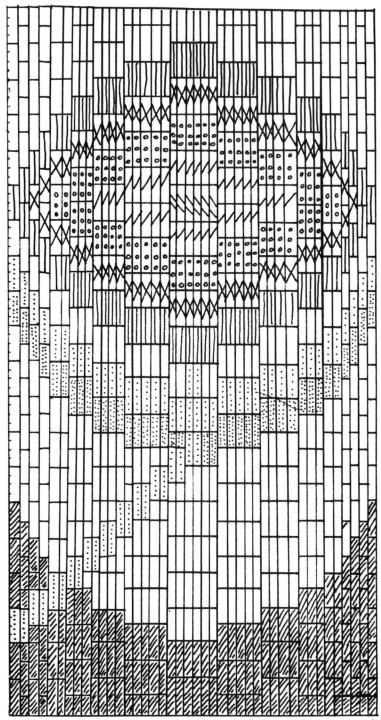

BEGINNING OF
NEXT FLOWER
UNIT

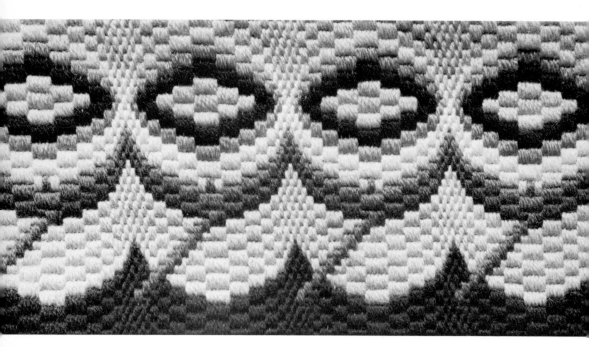

View of the completed stitching showing four flowers

sian yarn, so all three were used, with a richly textured surface resulting. To stitch it, you'll need a full skein of pale blue, two-thirds of a skein of brown, and varying lesser amounts of two greens, white, pink, maroon, yellow, and a bit of light orange. The flowers can be made in fewer colors if you don't have any small amounts of yarn on hand. You'll also need a clean, empty coffee can and some felt if you want to line it. This pattern fits most standard coffee cans, but you should check it out, using a paper pattern, before you start to stitch. The added bulk of the yarn also causes some shrinkage after stitching, so be sure to allow for this if you have to change the pattern.

Cut out the canvas and mark the outlines as shown. As this is a variation of a Bargello pattern, work it from the chart as many times as you need to, to fill in your outline. As shown, with the 14-mesh canvas, there were four and one-quarter flowers in the complete pattern. To make it more attractive at the side joining, the design was centered on the canvas as described in the Bargello chapter, and when it was completed, the two small parts of flowers on either end fit together, even though they did not complete a flower.

To work the design, do the outermost section of the flower, which is white in the one shown, to set it up, doing the lower row first and then the top to complete the outlined oval. Work the light green next, for the stem and top half of the leaves, then the dark green for the bottom half of the leaves. You can do the rest as it suits you, since the pattern follows regularly once the flower outlines and stems are stitched. Each time you reach the stem when working the background, do half stitches as needed to keep the pattern correct. You'll also need to do half stitches along the top and bottom for a straight edge, as usual in Bargello. You'll probably not need to block this, due to the type of stitches used.

To assemble, cut out a lining and bottom from the felt as shown. Trim the canvas to an inch all around. Cut slits along the bottom edge every inch or so, almost up to the stitching area. Fold the left-hand side of the canvas under and glue it in place with a thin line of white glue. Let dry. Place the stitching face down and put the coffee can on top of it. Run a line of glue along the top of the can, the canvas on the right side of the stitching, and the bottom of the can. Roll the canvas around the can, smoothing it in place and bring the left glued edge of the canvas up to the right edge which is now in place on the can. Add some glue to the right edge's canvas and smooth the left edge down on top of it. Make sure that the stitches along each edge match up correctly. Then fold the bottom onto the glued bottom of the can. Overlap the cut canvas so that it will lie flat on the bottom of the can and add more glue if needed to keep it in place. Put a line of glue around the edge of the circle of felt and place it smoothly over the glued canvas on the bottom of the can. Sit the can on its bottom, after it has dried. Spread glue around the inner edge of the can near the top and fold down the remaining canvas of the top of the stitchery. If you're adding the lining, wait until the glue dries and try it out inside the can to be sure that it fits. Then, add a line of glue around the edges of the lining and place it in the can and smooth it in place.

Quick point pillow. Designed and stitched by Katherine Komaroff.

Quick Point Pillow

This pillow is made out of rug yarn on 5-mesh penelope canvas. You'll need eight skeins of yarn, one each in white, light blue, medium blue, lavender, medium purple, pale yellow, light gold, and dark gold or pale orange. You can use fewer colors if you like, but part of the beauty of this pillow is the fine selection of colors, used in a growth pattern. The canvas should be at least 10 inches by 20 inches. Follow the chart for the design.

Mark the canvas, stitch in the design shown, and block. Cut a lining and stitch it to the pillow front with the right sides facing, stitching all four corners and three sides, leaving one short side open for turning right side out and stuffing. Stitch the opening closed after stuffing. If you want to add tassels as shown, use the remaining yarn.

To make each tassel, use as close to a quarter of whatever amount of each color that you have left so that the tassels are colored evenly. Cut out a piece of cardboard, the height of the tassel, in this case 3½ inches. Make it wide enough to handle easily. Wrap each color of yarn around the board, starting with the end of yarn at the bottom of the board and ending

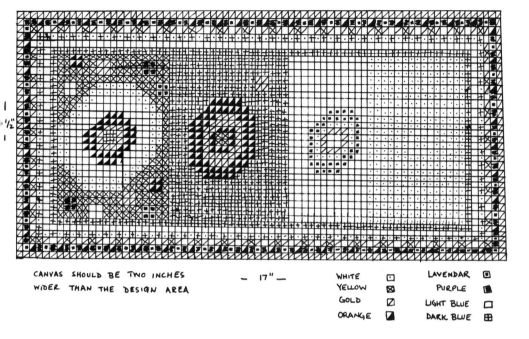

— 17" —

WHITE	⊡	LAVENDAR	◉
YELLOW	⊠	PURPLE	◼
GOLD	◪	LIGHT BLUE	☐
ORANGE	◤	DARK BLUE	⊞

Diagram of quick point pillow

off after you've wrapped about a quarter of the yarn of each color by bringing the yarn to the bottom of the board and cutting it there. Never end off the yarn at the top edge because it will pull out of the finished tassel and make a too-long end. Then, cut a piece of yarn seven inches long and slide it under the wrapped yarn on the cardboard and move it up to the top edge so that half of the yarn is on either side of the wrapped yarn. Tie it tightly in a double knot and smooth the ends down along with the rest of the yarn. Slip a scissors blade into the wrapped yarn at the bottom of the cardboard and cut through the yarn right at the edge. Cut another piece of yarn, six inches long, and tie it around the cut pieces of yarn, an inch below the center, where they are tied together. Make a tight double knot and smooth the ends of yarn into the rest of the tassel, trimming them if needed so that they are even. Do the same three more times, so that you have four tassels. Sew them onto the four corners of the pillow with a needle and strong thread.

Cross Stitch Drawstring Bag

This drawstring bag should be made out of a sturdy fabric, such as canvas, sailcloth, or denim, so that you will be sure of its strength. Half a yard of the fabric will be enough for the bag. If you want to add a lining you'll need half a yard of cotton or other lighter weight fabric. You'll also need some embroidery floss for the design and a small piece of fabric for the appliques that form part of the design. Any fabric of a color that

Left: Drawstring bag

How to stitch an applique

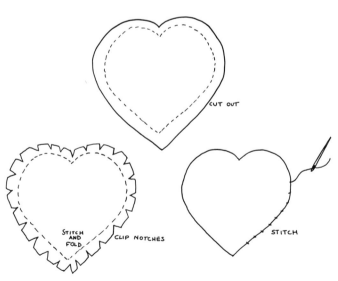

152

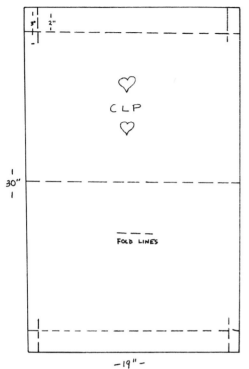

3" 2"

30"

C L P

FOLD LINES

− 19" −

Dimensions, fold lines, and stitch-
ing area of bag

appeals to you will be good for an applique, as long as it's not too hard to work with. You can use felt if you like, which is the easiest fabric for an applique. The colors are up to you.

Cut out the fabric in the dimensions shown. Mark the design lightly on the top half of the right side of the fabric. Cut out the appliques. If you use felt, you can cut it to size and stitch it in place, with an invisible overcast stitch. If you use a fabric that will unravel, cut out the applique ¼ inch larger on all sides. Then stitch a running stitch with regular sewing thread the same color as the applique, or two strands of the floss, on the original outlines of the applique, ¼ inch in from its cut edge. Then clip small V-shaped notches in the ¼ inch allowance and fold it down to the wrong side. If it doesn't stay in place easily, you can iron it. Then stitch it in place with an overcast stitch as shown. Cross stitch the rest of the design. Steam if needed.

To assemble the bag itself, sew it with strong thread or use a sewing

Stitch diagram for design on the front of the bag

machine. When sewing by hand, use a backstitch. At the uppermost ends of the long edges, fold under a ½ inch of fabric for about three inches. Stitch in place, at the tops of all four edges. Then make a fold two inches down from each short end and stitch to the wrong side of the fabric, as indicated by the fold lines in the pattern diagram. The stitching should be about ¾ inch from the end of the fabric after it is folded, to give you a long open-ended hem at the end of the fabric. After stitching both shorter ends the same way, turn the right sides of the fabric so that they face each other, folding the fabric in half so that the two hemmed edges meet at the top. Stitch up both sides, ending off the stitching at the line of stitching for the top hem. Add another seam for strength. If you're adding a lining, make it now by cutting it from the fabric to the same measurements as the bag itself, less two inches in length. Fold it in half with the right sides facing in and stitch up the two sides. Turn it right side out and slip it onto the stitched bag. Fold the top edge in to the wrong side. Stitch it with an overcast stitch to the line of stitching in the top of the bag that's holding the folds in place.

Turn the bag right side out. Make two drawstrings, each about 28 inches long, out of decorative cord, braided yarn, or light-weight, nicely woven rope. After you cut two lengths of the material that you've chosen, put a large safety pin at the end of one of them and slip it into the opening at the end of one top hem of the bag. Inch it through, using the pin to slide up in the folded tube of fabric. When you've finished on one side, take it to the opening of the other side and bring it through that one. When it reaches its other end, tie the two ends together an inch or two in from their ends. Do the same with the other drawstring, but start it on the other side so that when it is threaded through both sides, you have a knotted drawstring coming out of each side of the bag. Pull on both strings at the same time and there's your finished drawstring bag. If the drawstrings now seem too large, you can cut them down a bit and retie the ends. You can plan this bag larger or smaller as you wish, for a handy carryall, once you know how to make the basic size and shape.

NEEDLEPOINT AND EMBROIDERY SUPPLIERS—MAIL ORDER

Herrschners
Hoover Road
Stevens Point, Wisconsin 54481

LeeWards
Creative Crafts Center
P. O. Box 903
1200 St. Charles Street
Elgin, Illinois 60120

Merribee Needlecraft Company
P. O. Box 9680
2904 West Lancaster
Fort Worth, Texas 76107

The Needlecraft Shop
4501 Van Nuys Boulevard
Sherman Oaks, California 91403

Selma's Art Needlework
1645 Second Avenue
New York, New York 10028

Stitchcraft
4 Station Plaza
Glen Head, New York 11545

INDEX